GW00643162

MORE WORDS

OF

FAITH, HOPE, AND LOVE.

MORE WORDS

OF

FAITH, HOPE, AND LOVE

BEING

𝔏etters and 𝔈xtracts from 𝔏etters

WRITTEN BY

THE LATE JOHN DICKIE, OF IRVINE, SCOTLAND,

TO HIS FRIEND AND BROTHER IN CHRIST,

JAMES TODD, DUBLIN,

"The law of the Lord is perfect, converting the soul: the testimony of the Lord is sure, making wise the simple. The statutes of the Lord are right, rejoicing the heart: the commandment of the Lord is pure, enlightening the eyes The fear of the Lord is clean, enduring for ever: the judgments of the Lord are true and righteous altogether. More to be desired are they than gold, yea, than much fine gold: sweeter also than honey and the honeycomb. Moreover by them is Thy servant warned: and in keeping of them there is great reward."—Ps. xix. 7-11.

October, 1987
Published by
GOSPEL TRACT PUBLICATIONS
411 Hillington Road, Glasgow G52 4BL, Scotland

ISBN 0 948417 16 1

Printed by
GOSPEL TRACT PUBLICATIONS
411 Hillington Road, Glasgow, Scotland G52 4BL

PREFACE.

HAVING received communications from many persons testifying to the spiritual profit and blessing which they derived from the perusal of the former volume of the late Mr. John Dickie's letters, " Words of Faith, Hope, and Love, from the chamber of a Dying Saint," I am encouraged to publish this second volume.

All the letters in the first were written during Mr. Dickie's last long and trying illness, when for eight years of almost entire seclusion, and in constant weakness and suffering, he so experienced the all-sufficient grace of his loving God and Father, that he could triumphantly write of these years as " the cream of his whole life ; " and many tried and suffering believers who read this testimony of God's sustaining grace, have been encouraged to trust more completely than before in the love and faithfulness of their Heavenly Father.

But the letters, and extracts from letters, in this volume were written during a much more extended period, and were occupied with various subjects of the utmost practical importance. In publishing them, I thought it better to avoid the epistolary form, and classify them as far as possible. In some cases a letter is occupied with a special subject, and it forms a chapter by itself; while, in other cases, passages are selected from a number of letters, and are placed under one head, to help the reader to his edification. I should add that I have included a few passages from letters written by Mr. Dickie to another Christian friend.

I trust the reader will kindly remember that the writer of these letters had no idea that they ever would be published. They were simply the expression of his thoughts on subjects which we were from time to time considering together; having, however, myself derived much instruction and help from them, and thankful that so many were profited through the reading of the first volume of his letters, I now publish this second volume, with the earnest desire and prayer that God may be pleased to use the truths contained in it, also, for the edification, comfort, and instruction in righteousness of many of His children. And if He is graciously pleased thus to grant His blessing, I shall be abundantly compensated for whatever labour I have had in arranging it for publication, which indeed has been to me a labour of love.

JAMES TODD.

54 UPPER SACKVILLE STREET,
    DUBLIN.

CONTENTS.

CHAPTER I.

CHAPTER II.

CHAPTER X.

CHAPTER XI.

CHAPTER XII.

CHAPTER XIII.

CHAPTER XIV.

CHAPTER XV.

CHAPTER XVI.

CHAPTER XVII.

CHAPTER XXIV.

CHAPTER XXV.

CHAPTER XXVI.

CHAPTER XXXII.—*continued.*

CHAPTER XXXIII.

CHAPTER XXXIII.—*continued.*

CHAPTER XXXIV.

CHAPTER XXXV.

CHAPTER XXXVI.

MORE WORDS OF FAITH.

CHAPTER I.

GOD'S LOVE TO US.

1. GOD IS LOVE.

WHAT a matchless theme is this! May the
Holy Spirit guide and elevate our meditation. It is the loftiest, the most ravishingly
delightful, to which created intelligence ever has
been, or ever shall be, turned. It shall fully
occupy all the faculties of all the glorified through-
out eternity.

And to a heart attuned to the harmonies of
heaven, what a delightful study is here—the love
of God! It is the most wonderful fact known to
us; and we are so constituted that wonderful
things give us pleasure. See how men traverse
every ocean, and explore every continent; how

they dig into the earth, and mount above the clouds; and all in eager pursuit of the wonderful! It is a poor mind which is not capable of delight from the gratification of this faculty of wonder. But in this love of God to sinful man lies a greater wonder than all the marvels in creation put together. This is the cluster of wonders which the angels explore. They desire to look into it, for they find in it all the hidden treasures of wisdom and knowledge; and while they wonder at the love of God to man surely they must wonder, too, at the cold return we make to this amazing love. He loves us with His whole heart, and it is love on the same pitch that He looks for from us.

But it should intensify our delight in exploring the breadth, and length, and depth, and height of this love, a thousandfold, when we realise it as resting undivided upon our individual selves. His natural gifts He distributes, so that sometimes what one receives, another wants; but His love He lavishes entire and undiminished on every child He has. It is so even with an earthly parent. Tell me, O fondly - loving mother, whether thou assignest a measured portion of thy love to each of thy little ones, careful to divide it aright? Oh, never, never! Thou wert no mother if thou couldst act in this way. You bestow the entire total of your fervent mother-love on every child that nestles beside you. If we then, being evil, are constrained to act thus, how much more may we expect it from our heavenly Father, whose nature and whose name is Love.

And what is it, who is it, that God thus loves? If we should ask, with anxiety—But can God love the sinful? what a satisfactory reply does the life and death of Jesus give us! Oh, my brother, whatever we doubt, whatever we believe, let us be well assured of this, that our sin has not in the least abated the most tender love of God towards us (see Eph. ii. 4). Nay, the second creation, the crowning glory of the Almighty's works, was undertaken expressly with the object of manifesting to an adoring, delighted universe the exceeding riches of the love of God (Eph. ii. 5, 7). The first creation, on the apex of which the angels stand, was meant to exhibit His wisdom, power, and general goodness; but this second creation is designed to show forth the magnificence of Divine love.

But, though God loves the sinner, He does not, He cannot, He never will, love sin. He hates it with His whole heart, and with His whole soul.

His hatred of it admits of no increase. He cannot look upon it. And this hatred of sin is as much an essential characteristic of His nature as is His love to His creatures. For sin is no creature of His: He had no hand in the making of it, and He will never countenance it. So far from being His creature, sin would blast and destroy creation—it would turn the universe into one wide hell of horrors. But, just because God is love, He cannot endure sin. Its power is immense; but Omnipotence has declared a war of extermination against it; and, if it were not so, better far there had been no creation at all.

On every side the glorious *manifestations* of this Divine love are to be seen; and they who look abroad with anointed eyes are dazzled with the joyous vision. The Bible is filled with them; they sparkle on every page. Rightly read, the Bible is, like the Song of Solomon, a book of love. The world is equally filled with them. Sometimes we are ready to say the earth is full of sin and misery; but it is better to say with David: " The earth, O Lord, is full of Thy mercy." Sin, indeed, fearfully aboundeth; but there is something that is more abundant than even sin; for where sin abounded, grace did much more abound. And

Providence is filled with these manifestations. Everything that God does is done in love—nay, in infinite love. And what is it that this love will not stoop to? See the stable and the manger ; see the upper-room and the feet-washing ; see the agony in the garden, and the shame in the judgment-hall ; see the awful Cross and the sepulchre of Joseph. And though He is not now showing His love in acts identical with these—they are not now needed—He is still acting daily in precisely the same infinite love.

And the life of every Christian is filled with the tokens of this love. From the tender kiss with which the joyous father welcomed his returning prodigal, onward till the bestowal of the crown of glory, the entire course of the saint has been through love unutterable. And heaven is filled with the trophies of this love. Think of such sinners, snatched from such a depth, raised to such a height ; and all this with an expenditure of love that strikes one dumb.

In view of all this, how loving should we be ! and this, first, towards God. Oh, what response to a love like this ought to rise up continually from our most loving hearts ! God craves our poor love, and yearns for it ; for love cannot but desire to have its love returned. Indeed, it is the only gift we can give Him which He puts any value on. Without love, all worship, all ostensible service is nothing. " My son, give me thine heart." Oh, my brother, would you give joy to God? You will do so if you accept His love, and devote yourself to the one aim of returning it worthily.

And, besides this, how should we love our fellows? Indeed, if we do not, we have no love to God. We are not merely the objects of all this infinite love of God, but we are appointed to be its organs and its instruments in its working out the blessing of all around us. Oh, what manner of persons should WE be who are left in this world of sin and sorrow, to be the channels of outflow through which the immense love of God may empty its stores, flooding with blessings the parched hearts beside us! The Father sacrificed His Son for them—the Son sacrificed Himself. What art thou sacrificing for the same lost ones? Is it *little*? Is it NOTHING? If so, how unlike we are to God or to His Christ; how unlike to one who is being led by the Spirit!

2. GOD'S LOVE—MAN'S HATRED.

OH, what a marvellous story of love, and of hatred, is set before us in the life, and especially in the death of the Lord Jesus ! " Herein, indeed, is love," herein, too, is hatred—God's unutterable love to sinful man, man's unutterable hatred to the Holy God (John xv. 23, 24, 25). Could love, even Divine love, do more ? Could hatred do more ? We see so clearly in it all what God's nature is—even Holy LOVE, and that love INFINITE (1 John iv. 8). We see, too, what man's horrible nature now is, as utterly fallen—how he hates this Holy God " with ALL his heart, and soul, and strength, and mind." Is it not glorious to see this on the one side, is it not heartrending to see it on the other ? OUR perfectly irreconcilable hatred to God (Rom. viii. 7, 8) is such that we would KILL Him if *we* could ; and we have actually done the nearest to this that could be done—when we murdered the incarnate Son of God *when He came to bring us all the riches of the Father's love.* And such is God's love, that He has actually done what comes as near as could be to this : for His co-equal Son took flesh on Him that He might die for us, and all this in pure and fervent love for the creatures who hated and who murdered Him.

There is, in this strange story of love and of
hatred, that which breaks one's heart to dwell on
it, and also that which heals the heart which has
been thus broken. It gives us such a sight of *ourselves* as makes us ashamed and silent (Ezek.
xvi. 63), while it gives us such a sight of God as
fills us with a joy unspeakable (1 Peter i. 8).   Oh
for an ever-deepening sense of this guilty shame.
Oh for an increasing experience of this gladness !

For we must never forget that all this love is
love that God feels *for* OURSELVES, and that it is a
love that He feels for us *at this moment* as tenderly
as ever—a love which is busily arranging for us
EVERY circumstance of our lot, every day and every
hour.   And we must never forget that the hatred
to this God is a hatred that is in *your heart and*
MINE *at this very hour*.   It belongs to our fallen
nature, and the murder of the Son of God lies at
the door of every one who partakes of that nature ;
our carnal mind can feel towards God in no other
way than this : IT ALWAYS HATES HIM.   We are
told in Rom. viii. 7, 8, that it CANNOT be subject
to Him.

Into this most sinful nature we were born, and
in this nature we have lived, up till the time when,
receiving Christ *as our* ALL, we were made par-

takers of HIS *nature*, and began to put off our own (Eph. iv. 22, 24), and to crucify it—that is, kill it (Gal. v. 24). And while we lived in this nature ALL that we did was sin (see Rom. viii. 7, 8 ; also Rom. xiv. 23). And though ·no true Christian lives in this old nature, yet the old nature is still in us, and we must watch, and pray, and fight against it—else, alas, alas, the issue shall be very dreadful. See how Paul struggled against his old nature (1 Cor. ix. 27). For this old nature, which remains in us till death, never is and *never* CAN BE subject to God (Rom. viii. 7, 8). It is incurable. To the very end it HATES *God,* and would KILL HIM if *it could.*

Now, to apply all this in a few words, it is the very same unutterable love which led God to send His beloved Son to die for us, which leads Him *now* to send sorrows on you and on me. " As for ·God, His way is perfect "—perfect love, perfect wisdom (Ps. xviii. 30). On the other hand it is the same unutterable hatred which led our race to crucify the Son of God, which *now* tempts us to murmur at the will of God, and to wish we could get rid of it. For Jesus was just God, and the hatred which man felt towards God, he poured forth on His Son. And so, now, the will of God, the afflicting will of

God, IS JUST GOD; for it is the outcome of all that God is—it represents Him to us, just as Jesus did to the Jews; and the old nature in us, if we allowed it to rule, would lead us to indulge our natural hatred of God by dislike to His will.

But we have got another nature, even the very nature of Christ; and it is in this new nature that we are now to live. And this new nature, because it LOVES GOD with all its power of loving, loves also the WILL of God, whether it brings to us trouble or comfort. The very key-note of our new life is—what was the key-note of Christ's own life: " I came not to do mine own will, but the will of Him that sent me " (John vi. 38; Ps. xl. 8).

And though we cannot understand all the outs and ins of His wonderful plans about us, we *can* TRUST HIM, perfectly assured that He is doing everything that concerns us in infinite love, and in unerring wisdom. And besides this, let us surrender *our own* WILLS *altogether*, and let the fervent desire of our hearts now be, that HIS WILL be done, and *not ours*. And with this faith in our Father's love, and this entire acceptance of His holy will *in* EVERYTHING, our peace shall be a peace that passes all understanding (Phil. iv. 7).

3. GOD'S HATRED OF SIN, AND HIS LOVE
OF THE SINNER.

THE Gospel I take to be God's revelation of
HIMSELF through Christ Jesus, in respect to those
points which man needs to know, if he is to be
saved. These points are principally two—First,
That God INFINITELY HATES SIN ; and second, that
He INFINITELY LOVES the SINNER. The fact of this
love and this hatred we could only have guessed at,
had Ho not most clearly revealed it ; and, as for
the measure of both the love and the hatred, it
could not have entered our hearts to conceive. He
hates sin with HIS WHOLE heart, so that He could
not hate it more—*see the Cross of Jesus ;* He loves
the sinner with His whole heart, so that He could
not love him more—*see the Cross of Jesus.* It is
not merely that He is angry with the sin. Anger
may be pacified ; but this is HATRED — *heart-*
HATRED—the hatred of Him who is *infinite* and
UNCHANGEABLE.

But when I speak of sin, it is sin in the Bible
sense of the word, not *crime* or *vice* merely, but
such sin as the love of the world, and the selfish
enjoyment of its good things, the pleasure we enjoy
when our vanity or pride or ambition is gratified ;

in short, everything we do, even eating and drinking, if it is not done out of love to God, and with a desire to please Him (see *Rom.* xiv. 23). Now all this sin of living for self, God hates unutterably; so hates it, that He cannot endure it.

But then, along with this, the Gospel tells us that God loves OURSELVES — loves us tenderly, infinitely, so loves us that He gave His Son to save us from our sins (John iii. 16). And we need to know BOTH of these truths. The first alone, and by itself, would sink us to utter despair. The last alone would lead us into fatal presumption. But the two together, put us and keep us in the right position of HUMBLE TRUST. Oh, how trustful should we be! Oh, how we need to believe these two halves of the Gospel! By believing, I don't mean the mere assent to them; but the hearty realisation of the two tremendous facts of God's hatred of sin—and His love to us sinners. And that they should be so true to us that our entire lives may be shaped by them, that we do what we do, and leave undone what we leave undone, just because we know and believe this wonderful Gospel of God's holiness and love. This is true faith. And this faith shall most assuredly change our own characters completely. We too shall be led by it

to abhor sin, which God abhors ; while we love and
trust and obey the loving Holy One, who in love
has redeemed us for Himself by the blood of His
Son.

---

4. LOVE OF THE FATHER, SON, AND HOLY SPIRIT.

ALL creation is one immense manifestation of
stupendous love, redemption is an unspeakably
more wonderful exhibition of love on a still grander
scale. Providence, though we are not able to
trace its marvels, is nothing but love. And glory
shall be love made perfect, when the saint shall
love even as he is beloved. For God is love.
Father, Son, and Holy Ghost. Whom does the
Father love ? Even this sinful, lost, and wicked
world—a world that hated, and still hates Him
(John xv. 24 ; Rom. i. 30). And how much does
He love this wicked race ? So much that He gave
His dearly beloved Son to the agonies of that
wonderful life and death to save us (see John iii.
16). And the Son loves, but whom does He love ?
Even ME, EVEN ME. And how much does He love
me ? So much that He gave Himself for me (Gal.
ii. 20). And the Holy Spirit loves—loves us just
as tenderly as either the Father or the Son, for the

three are ONE. Oh, when we look with faith, we
can see that we are surrounded with, plunged into
the deep profundities of an ocean of Divine love.
The arms of love are spread out beneath us (Deut.
xxxiii. 27).   Loving arms clasp us to the loving
bosom (Song ii. 6).   On this loving bosom Jesus
lays us to rest, in perfect peace (Isa. xl. 11 ; xxvi.
3).   Above us floats a banner of love (Song ii. 4),
and round about us crowd hosts on hosts of
unnumbered mercies on every side (Ps. xxxii. 10).

May the Lord reveal more of the wonders of His
love to us by His Holy Spirit, and increase our
enjoyment of them.   And we may rest assured in
view of all this wonderful grace, that having such a
Father, He will do all that love and wisdom can
devise for His helpless child.   And it is the place
of one, who is the child of such a Father, to lie
meekly and quietly in the Father's hand, trusting
Him utterly, and obeying Him implicitly.

———

5. "THE LORD THINKETH ON ME."

WHAT a golden word; it is seldom out of my
mind.   Since He is lovingly thinking of us (Psa.
xl. 17), what matters it who forgets us ?   And

these thoughts of God about us are beyond all counting (ver. 5); and they are most precious (Ps. cxxxix. 17, 18). And no wonder these thoughts are innumerable; God has been thinking of you and of me, all down through the BYPAST ETERNITY; and so many, and so grand, are His thoughts, that it will take the WHOLE OF THE ETERNITY TO COME to afford time to work them out. And how gracious are all these thoughts, worthy of Him whose nature and whose name is LOVE. One of these thoughts was, that He would give us Christ, with all His fulness of grace and glory, for our eternal portion. Another thought was that He would give us His OWN SPIRIT, to dwell within us for ever, the source of a holy Christ-like life. Another was that He would give Himself to us, as to be actually our Father; and that He would lay us in His very *bosom*, as His dearest children—that bosom in which never lay angel, or any other, saving His only-begotten Son (John i. 18; xiii. 25; xvii. 23, 26). And all His thoughts about us are on this tremendous scale; while they are more in number than the sand on the sea-shore (Ps. cxxxix. 17, 18). Yes, indeed, it will take the ENDLESS ETERNITY to carry them into effect.

6. THE FATHER'S TENDER LOVE.

THERE is nothing that is beyond His power to do for us—nothing above His wisdom to contrive for us—nothing outside of His resources to supply us. And all His power, His wisdom, His resources, are at the disposal of His deep hearty love for ourselves as His own dear children—a love which not only comes up to the height of an earthly father's, or an earthly mother's love, but goes infinitely beyond it. And this love has been exerting itself for our benefit, with all its tenderness and fervency, during all our past lives—is acting still, and will go on to love us, and watch over us, and bless us FOR EVER. Do we really believe all this ? If we do, we ought never to doubt that God's heart towards us is that of a tender Father, and living from hour to hour in the ASSURED FAITH of it, we are to look to Him for everything. Now, the new-born babe is not left to earn its food, or to buy it, or to choose what it shall be, or to cook it. The parent most lovingly cares for all that, the helpless babe has only to take it; so with the feeding of a spiritual soul. God will look after it well; only the man must leave it all with God (1 Peter ii. 2).

7. IMMEASURABLE LOVE.

WHAT a satisfying portion the Lord Jesus is, with all the unsearchable riches of His love, and of His sweet communion! Let us try to search out the unsearchable wonders of His grace and His glory; to measure the immeasurable lengths, and breadths, and depths, and heights of His infinite love. We cannot do it! Well, but let us try our utmost, just that we may find out that it cannot bo done; and that we cannot do it, not because we are so very small, but because Christ and His fulness of grace is so inconceivably great. And now, when we have worn out ourselves with our unsuccessful effort to comprehend Him, let us refresh our weary hearts with the delightful thought that this same Christ, with ALL that He is, and ALL that He has, and ALL that He can do, is actually God's amazing gift of love to us. Yes, God has given us His beloved Son, because He SO LOVED us, that no smaller gift would have sufficed to express the greatness of that love. We need nothing more.

---

8. PERFECT LOVE GIVES ALL.

THE Lord Jesus in His love keeps back nothing
from thee : He COULD NOT DO IT, He is constantly
giving ; He gives thee His ALL ; He has given
thee His VERY SELF. It is more delightful for
Him to give to thee, than for thee to get. At this
moment, the Lord Jesus in heaven has no more
than thou hast upon earth, for, in purest love, He
shares His ALL with thee, His sonship (John i. 12);
His glory (John xvii. 22); and at length His very
throne (Rev. iii. 21). For PERFECT LOVE does not,
and CANNOT keep any thing back from its beloved,
and thou art the object of His PERFECT LOVE.
Heaven would be greatly wanting to Him without
His people beside Him ; therefore He is coming to
receive them to Himself. What a shocking thing
that any of us should seek or find our rest on this
sin-cursed earth without HIM !

CHAPTER II.

OUR LOVE TO GOD.

1. GOD MADE US FOR LOVE.

THE secret of a holy, happy life is whole-hearted love to the Lord Jesus. We shall delight in His full, free love, only in so far as we ourselves love Him. We never value the love of anyone unless we love them. Now, God made us for love. We have fallen from this condition of love, down, down into a state of selfishness; and in this selfishness lie our sin and our misery. For all that selfishness does is a sin; and all that selfishness can accomplish is misery. But now, in recovering us, God has redeemed us for a life of pure love, and in regeneration has made us partakers of the Divine nature—(2 Peter i. 4)—which is LOVE; and He has given us His own Spirit to strengthen us to walk as Christ walked, which is the Spirit of LOVE and of power (2 Tim.

i. 7). Heaven is what it is because it is the home
of perfect love ; and hell is hell, because it is filled
with ripened selfishness. For happiness can enter
no heart, except through the doorway of LOVE.

In connection with all this I am greatly touched
with the words in Eph. v. 1, 2. We are called on
to IMITATE God ; and this because we are beloved
children ; and, as such, are partakers of His nature.
We are called on further, to reproduce in our own
lives this wonderful life of Christ ; and this in its
manifestation of a love unto the death. Oh, what
a lofty mission ! God is LOVE, infinite, unutterable
LOVE ; and, while the Christian is to consider
himself the object of all this inconceivable wealth
of love, he is equally to look on himself as its
anointed instrument. Oh, my beloved friend, God
has set YOU and ME down in the midst of sinful
and miserable men and women, who are sinful
and miserable because they know not, believe not,
realise not the love of God. And God has set us
down among them that we might be both witnesses
to them of this love, and also its willing, its self-
sacrificing organs. God wants to pour out on
them that love of His through our hearts, and
hands, and lips, and eyes. What a calling is this
for dust and ashes like us ! We are set apart and

anointed as really as Jesus was, though on a lower
level, to manifest the holy love of God to sinful
men; and to do this so clearly, that though they
have no eyes that can see God, or His love, they
may be able to catch a faint glimpse of it by
seeing us and our lives of Christ-like LOVE.

You cry, "But who is sufficient for such a life?"
I reply that you and I are sufficient, if we be
believing and faithful. God has called us to it;
and to fit us for it, Christ Himself is now living
and acting WITHIN us. Our lives are meant to be
such that we shall be able to explain them only by
saying: It is not I that live it; it is Christ who
dwelleth in me (Gal. ii. 20).

2. DESIRES AFTER GOD.

GOD always quickens desires after grace before
He bestows it. Blessed are they whose desires
after God and His grace are like the pangs of
starvation (see Matt. v. 6). Notice how David
thus hungered (Ps. xlii. 1, 2; also Ps. lxiii. 1;
also Ps. lxxxiv. 1, 2; and most of all in Ps.
cxix. 20, when he says his heart *actually* BROKE
with its longing). Again he says, "I opened my

mouth and panted" (Ps. cxix. 131). And it is
when we open our mouths wide in this way that
God fills them (Ps. lxxxi. 10). For He delights to
fill the hungry with His best good things, but the
rich—the full of enjoyments—He sends empty
away, as Mary sings in her most lovely song of
praise (Luke i. 53). Nay, it is when we seek God
with OUR WHOLE HEART, that we have the promise
of finding Him (Jer. xxix. 13). For as He deals
with the parched earth, so He does also with the
soul of man. He first makes the earth to desire
rain, and then He pours on it the full river of God,
that is, the full rain clouds (see Ps. lxv. 9, with
the margin reading).

Oh, then we ought to seek Christ more and
more, and still more eagerly. Let Him be so
much to us, that we shall need no more, shall
desire no more to fill up our cup of enjoyment to
the very brim. David (whose intense desires we
have just seen) says of his cup, " My cup runneth
over" (Ps. xxiii. 5). And well he might, for the
Lord Himself was in the cup, and that made it too
full to hold what it contained.

And what encouragement it is to us to desire,
and to seek, and to expect sweet communion with
Him, when we remember that the communion of

a believing, loving soul, is far sweeter to Him than it is to us. He says to the bride, " How fair is thy love, My sister, My spouse! how much better is thy love than wine, and the smell of thine ointments than all spices " (see Song of Sol. iv. 10). And the bride resting in the love of her Lord can say with secret gladness, " I am my beloved's, and HIS DESIRE *is towards* ME " (Song of Sol. vii. 10).

3. THE BLESSEDNESS OF LOVING GOD.

WILL you permit me to say to you what I am constantly urging on my own heart, and that is, to seek as one seeks for NOTHING else, to be filled with the fullest possible measure of love to God. It is this love which constitutes holiness, and which floods the soul with joy. We should meditate often and deeply on the glories of the Divine character, as so clearly revealed in the lovely face of Jesus, and also on other themes fitted to foster this love ; and to all, add prayer for it WITHOUT CEASING, remembering that our Heavenly Father is infinitely more ready to bestow than we to ask. With far more loving readiness than any mother ever gave her breast to her starving child, does He give the Holy Spirit, the Creator of this love, to all who ask (Luke xi. 13).

As we love God, just as much and no more shall His love to us be our unspeakable delight ; for unless we love any one, we care nothing for his love to ourselves. Just as we love God, shall all His providential dealings, whether afflicting or comforting, bring a ceaseless joy to us; for, if we love God, we shall be perfectly pleased with all that He does. Just as we love Him shall duty be a pleasure, worship an exquisite enjoyment, and self-denial sweeter than any self-indulgence could be. Just as we love Him shall earth become like heaven ; this waste, howling wilderness shall be lovelier to our vision than Eden was—it shall be a Holy of Holies, filled on all sides with the tokens of our Father's majestic presence. Let us then seek, importunately SEEK this love; and just as we open our mouths wide for it will He fill them (Ps. lxxxi. 10). The Lord direct our hearts into the love of God (2 Thess. iii. 5).

----

4. LOVE TO THE LORD JESUS.

IN order to provoke our poor cold hearts to the love of Christ, shall we try to meditate a little on

His love. What a delightful word is that in
Galatians ii. 20 : "Who loved ME, and gave Himself
for ME." Oh, let our faith cling to this wonderful fact with the grip of a drowning man. And
how wonderful is this love of the Lord Jesus to
loathsome creatures like you and me. It is
wonderful in the fact of it ; still more so in the
intensity of it. And how delightful is it to appropriate it, and to rest in it, and to sing for gladness
of heart, in the assured belief that Christ hath
loved ME, and given Himself for me. His love had
no beginning, and shall have no end (Jer. xxxi. 3).

How sweet is love ; how inexpressibly sweet.
Nothing earthly is half so sweet. It is sweet to be
loved ; but it is far sweeter to love. And, in regard
to communion with Christ in love, we have the joy
of both these sweetnesses ; for we both get love and
give it. We get it up to Christ's capacity for
giving us love ; and we give it up to our capacity
for loving, when that capacity is enlarged to the
utmost by the Holy Spirit. Oh, what a life of
heaven-like joy is a life of fellowship with Christ
in love ! His love is not only sweet in itself, but
it sweetens EVERYTHING to us. It can make
bodily affliction sweet ; and can make death
delightful. Let us keep looking unto Jesus. Let

Christ be everything to us. The very feeblest, timid glance of trust that ever was cast on Him by a sin-oppressed soul, is infinitely more acceptable to God, and infinitely more helpful to ourselves, and infinitely more powerful in producing in our hearts love to the Lord Jesus, than ALL the religiousness of men acting in their own energies. For this glance effects a vital union between the soul and the Saviour which no labours or feelings of our own can do, and without which there can be no love to God. And as often as this feeble glance of faith is repeated the spiritual union between Christ and the soul is made closer and stronger; not closer and stronger on Christ's side of it—for on His side it was perfect from the beginning—but on our side of it. Oh, then, let us look and look, and keep looking, for we live and love by looking unto Jesus (2 Cor. iii. 18).

CHAPTER III.

POVERTY OF SPIRIT.

1. The First of the Beatitudes.

DIVINE truth, as God has revealed it to us, is a most skilfully compounded medicine, perfectly adapted by the unerring Physician to the case of the sick one under care. When received, *as He administers it,* how powerful, but how searching! It sinks us down to the very lowest; it lifts us up to the highest heights. It empties us of all that the self-life cares one rush for; it fills us to overflowing out of "all the fulness of God."

What an instructive portraiture of a true disciple is set before us by our Lord in that wonderful discourse of His on the Mount (Matt. v. 3–10). He draws it for us in seven striking features; and the very *first* of these is: POVERTY OF SPIRIT. This is *the* FIRST in the order of time, and also of importance. For it is the root out of which all the others grow. Till this be planted nothing further of a gracious kind is possible. When this is planted and watered, all the others grow out of it naturally (that is, according to the second nature) and necessarily, the deep poverty of spirit produces mourning before God (verse 4), and gentle, sweet meekness of spirit towards men (verse 5), and hungerings and thirstings INSATIABLE after a full conformity to the perfect will of God (verse 6), and so on to the end. And these resultant graces powerfully react on the first, the original grace ; for the increase of spiritual life discovers to the soul more and more of its enormous evils, and these discoveries deepen still further the deep poverty of soul which goes on to work a still profounder sorrow (verse 4), and a still gentler meekness (verse 5), and a still more eager hunger and thirst for holiness. And thus the work of grace is carried on in the soul. The Lord in the meantime comforting the sorrow, in measure at least (verse 4), and satisfying (though only in measure now) the "VEHEMENT DESIRE" (2 Cor. vii. 11) of the hungering soul (verse 6).

The first work, then, of the Holy Ghost, conviction of sin (John xvi. 8), in any heart tends to produce this deep poverty of spirit; and, evermore, as He leads the renewed soul into more abundant life (John x. 10), He leads it into a deeper and deeper self-abasement before God. Paul, who in A.D. 59 (I take the dates of the margin) counted himself to be unworthy of the *Apostolate* (1 Cor. xv. 19), had by A.D. 64 sunk so much lower in his poverty of spirit, that he now counted himself to be unworthy of being looked on *as a saint at all* — "LESS than THE LEAST among all the redeemed" (Eph. iii 8); while by A.D. 65 he had sunk so low as to feel himself unfit to be looked on as an *ordinary* SINNER—he was the ONE WORST OF ALL, and his case was a PATTERN CASE (1 Tim. i. 15, 16). Oh, my friend, this is the path along which all the divinely led are led to glory (Rom. viii. 14).

But while the Holy Spirit uses His own word and ordinances to carry on this deep work in the soul, man, left to himself, uses these for the very opposite purposes. God gave to Israel the law and the ordinances connected with it, to prepare Israel for the coming of His Son. Had they used that law and observed these ordinances with "good and honest hearts" (Luke viii. 15), they would have made them so far "poor in spirit," and "mourning" for sin, and meek, and "hungering for right-eousness," etc., etc., that they would have joyfully welcomed the promised Bringer of every blessing. But instead of this, they so used the law of God, that their one-sided perverse use of it brought the most religious among them to the state of soul represented in Luke xviii. 11, 12. The means designed to work in them poverty of soul, wrought only pride; and in their pride, they crucified the Lord of glory.

Of course, the law alone could not bring men to the full measure of true poverty of spirit. To accomplish this needs the clearer, fuller revelation which God has made of Himself in the Gospel. For this end is the Gospel given, that it may both humble us to the lowest, and exalt us to the very highest. And how overwhelming is this wonderful revelation, when it is received IN FAITH. What infinite holiness on the part of God! What infinite love! And what unutterable wickedness, desperate and inconceivable on the part of man! Rightly used, every element of Gospel truth breaks the hard heart to pieces, while it equally comforts and heals the heart that is thus broken. But its first opera-tion is to make one "poor in spirit." Alas, that there are so many who use the Gospel, just as the

Jews used the law, to produce the opposite spirit of a presumptuous rest in self. They do not glory indeed in their *legal* doings—this belonged to the *legal* dispensation; but they may glory in their *Gospel-believing*, which is the peculiar form that SELF-RIGHTEOUSNESS takes under a purely evangelical dispensation.

And while everything in the Word of God tends to produce and to deepen this holy poverty of spirit, does not everything in one's own experience operate in the same direction? For me, I can look back on nothing of my own, that, looked at in the light of God, does not abase me. Is it God's temporal goodness? how have I misused it! Is it His spiritual mercy? how little have I improved under it! Every recollection makes one groan with grief and shame, " That thou mayest *remember*, and be *confounded*, and never open thy mouth any more because of thy shame, WHEN I AM PACIFIED towards thee for ALL that thou hast done, saith the Lord God" (EZEKIEL xvi. 63). Verily, verily, one is of a truth the chief of sinners.

To be poor in spirit should be easy to us *as creatures*, should be easier far AS SINNERS, should be infinitely easy when we review our course AS CHRISTIANS—and yet, this poverty is impossible to us without special Divine help.

How astonishingly prone are we to be self-elated. See Hezekiah puffed up because of answered prayer (2 Chron. xxxii. 25). See the Jews "haughty" because of God's holy mountain (Zeph. iii. 11). See Paul in imminent danger, because he had been caught up into Heaven, and needing to correct this, the bitter medicine of sore Satanic sifting (2 Cor. xii. 7). See Laodicea wholly engulfed in it (Rev. iii. 14–17). Oh, my friend, I know not how you feel in view of all this; but as I now write, the recollection of my own past, and the consciousness of the present, fill me with feelings that are unutterable. I need to be " KEPT by the POWER of God;" blessed be His Name that He engages to keep every helpless one who commits his soul to Him for keeping (2 Tim. i. 12).

How patiently and persistently God labours with us, with me, I know, to work this poverty of spirit ! How would any one of us feel, if some fellow-creature who knew us altogether were to take us apart, and to set our faults before us in their infinity of number, and their shocking heinousness of aggravation ? As he went on, and on, with the endless story, it is certain that it would waken in us some sort of feeling ; and that this feeling would grow more intense, till it became unbearable. But, query, what would this intense feeling be ? Would it be that of penitent grief and shame, the deep and ever-deepening self-loathing of a broken-hearted man ? Or would the feeling be one of disgust and indignation, waxing hotter and more indignant, till, weary of restraint, it broke forth in fierce retorts ? Well, whether man may speak to me in this fashion or not, *God has been thus speaking to me*—in His Word, in His providence, by His Spirit. Do I break down completely under the awful revelation which He makes to me of MYSELF ? If I do not, then I must take one or other of two courses. I must either flare up, and protest, and rage, which there are not many who dare to do in the face of the Almighty, or, instead of this, I may close my ear and avert my heart, and become to His reproofs like a very deaf adder. For He has given to man—to all men — the marvellous capacity of silencing, for a season at least, the Almighty voice, of ignoring it as completely as if not one word were uttered. Alas, that this is the course so often taken by men, when the gracious God condescends to speak to them in mercy about their sins. It is the very

2:4

worst course of all, as it is also the commonest. By means of it, men too easily avoid the blessed humiliations of " poverty of spirit."

But what an infinite loss this is, even in regard to mere enjoyment, were there nothing more. If we could know of others all that we do know of ourselves, we could not love them ; while yet we manage to love ourselves, of whom we know so much that is evil. But God who knows us to be infinitely worse than we think, LOVES US NONE THE LESS. Oh, what must HIS love be, when He loves us even in a condition such, that our clear perception of it would fill us with *uttermost self-loathing.* We cling to the idolatry of self-love for sake of its *sweetness ;* but how *much sweeter* is it to cast it from us as a delusion and a fraud, and to find *all* our comfort in the FREE, holy, most wonderful love of God *in Christ.*

. And how this " poverty of spirit " helps us to discern and to delight in the perfect FREENESS of the grace of God, and the greatness of the merits of Christ ! How it strengthens the sense of our extreme *dependence* on Him for EVERY thing ! It quickens LOVE, on the principle of Luke vii. 47, for we love the more as we see how much we are forgiven. It deepens unspeakably the soul's intense

hatred of sin, and stirs up to increased watchfulness
against it. It strengthens the spirit of *self-denial*
—one of the grand points which is nearly forgotten
in this day of self-indulgence. It makes us meek
and gentle towards others. It increases joy in the
Lord, and the joy which it excites is *pure* and
simple joy *in Christ*—joy, in what He is, and is
TO ME (Gal. vi. 14). It casts us on the present
loving *intercession* of our Lord, a most indispensable part of His priestly office, which is unhappily
overlooked too much ; but which Paul places at the
very apex of the pyramid of blessings, naming it as
the highest and the last (Rom. viii. 34). In a
word, poverty of spirit is the first and most important stage in a TRUE REPENTANCE— repentance,
which is one of the absolute essentials to personal
salvation, and which constituted the one-half of the
Apostle's Gospel testimony (Acts xx. 21) ; but of
which our modern developments have robbed us so
much. Oh, we *cannot*, CANNOT have too high an
estimate of Christ's goodness, or too deep an estimate of our own badness ; and the one shall always
be in precise proportion to the other. High
thoughts of self mean low thoughts of Christ ;
worthy thoughts of Christ mean a most lowly
estimate of self. But in all this poverty of spirit

there is no slavish fear, no dread of wrath. The love which accompanies it, and the belief in God's infinite and FREE love, casts out the terror; but, oh, the humiliation and the sorrow—sorrow for having grieved the Spirit (Eph. iv. 30) and dishonoured our most loving Lord. And then our Heavenly Father sweetly comforts this sorrow (Matt. v. 4), and He goes on to satisfy, in measure, our vehement longings for increased conformity to His holy will, for every true grace enjoyed by us here is but the *partial* filling of some painfully-felt need (Matt. v. 6).

I know not, dear friend, what you may think of all this. For myself, I desire to ask the fullest measure of this poverty of spirit vouchsafed to man. Shall we ask this for one another? It is the *pledge* and the earnest of *every other* Spiritual blessing (Isa. lxvi. 2).

---

2. What I am not, yet ought to be.

It is not my doings, past or present, that trouble me most. So long as a man is taken up with these, he will never know himself. Neither is it WHAT I AM that troubles me most. The thing that grieves me, even to heart-break, is this: WHAT I AM NOT, while yet I SHOULD BE IT. It is this dreary margin, these miles on miles of waste, between what I ought to be and what I am not, that lays me in the dust, and makes me ofttimes feel that such a word as ABHOR myself is too feeble to express my feeling. Yet, out of all these humbling and heart-breaking experiences, come all my sweetest hours; such a frame of spirit God so loves, that He cannot keep out of the heart where He sees it; it is His choicest dwelling-place (Isa. lvii. 15). Of all the services which men render Him, there is no sacrifice so acceptable as to offer to Him a broken and contrite heart (Ps. li. 17).

CHAPTER IV.

REPENTANCE AND FAITH.

THE light, which shows us so consolingly the glory of God's grace in Christ Jesus, reveals to us also more distinctly than ever our own sinfulness. And while the one half of the Bible breaks the believing heart to pieces, the other half sweetly comforts and heals the broken heart. And this is not a mere act completed once for all, but a lifelong process, the breaking going on, and the healing also still going on.

I have been struck with the dissimilarity of the Gospel, as stated by Paul, and that stated by some of our modern preachers. Paul preached two things : repentance towards God, and faith towards the Lord Jesus Christ (see Acts xx. 21), while many in modern times quietly suppress the repentance altogether. You may also read many gospel tracts, and you will find the same thing—while you read a call to faith on every page, perhaps you will not once notice repentance hinted at.

Now, why is this? Not so did the Baptist preach (Matt. iii. 2, 11). Not so did the Lord Jesus preach (Matt. iv. 17; Matt. ix. 13; Luke xiii. 3, 5). Not so did the twelve preach during their Master's lifetime (Mark iv. 12). Neither were they so to preach after His ascension (Luke xxiv. 47). And they preached as He told them (Acts ii. 38; iii. 19; v. 31; xi. 18; xx. 21; xxvi. 20). Why then is repentance so little named to sinner or to saint nowadays? Oh, it is included in faith, someone says. No, not at all; it is a state of mind that has reference to God, while faith has reference to the Lord Jesus Christ. The one is distinct from the other, and neither includes its companion. I grant that the one implies the other; but that does not warrant that we drop the repentance, and testify to the faith alone, any more than it would warrant us to drop the faith, and testify simply to the repentance. We cannot truly repent towards God without also believing in the Lord Jesus; and as little can we truly believe in the Lord Jesus without also repenting towards God. How perilous, then, that experience which has so much to do with believing in Christ, but which, from beginning to end, knows so little about *repentance towards God*. And how unsatisfactory that mode of stating Gospel truth must be, which is so different from the mode in which Christ and His apostles taught it.

We have sinned, fearfully sinned, and that we may be delivered from it and its consequences, *two* things are needed—TWO and not *one*. The sinner must make *atonement* to God's outraged law for his sin, and make such sufficient atonement that it will be a righteous thing for God to accept the satisfaction in lieu of the sinner's actual punishment. And secondly, the sinner must also repent of his sin, confess it, bewail it, abhor it, and forsake it; and unless he does this, he still, of course, retains his sin. The first, namely, atonement, the sinner could not do, could not even help to do; so God sent forth His Son to be made sin for us, to accomplish full atonement by His precious blood. And FAITH lays hold *on* HIM, and rests sweetly ON HIM, and finds in His person and finished work all that it needs to put away the guilt of sin by making atonement for it. But there is the second thing, the actual putting away of the sin itself, and the being suitably exercised about it before God; and this is done by the sinner's REPENTANCE. This repentance, unlike the *atonement*, cannot be done for him, but must be done by himself, and *in his own bosom;* and as fallen nature cannot of itself repent, the same Son of God who has *on the Cross* and *without ourselves* made full atonement for us, has also procured for us, and supplies to us, the Holy Spirit, who, within us and with *our co-operation*, works genuine repentance towards God. By REPENTANCE, we *return to the God* whom we forsook ; by FAITH we come to Him, *through Christ the one and only way.* The two cannot be *separated,* though they are quite distinct. Rome separates them, and preaches repentance without faith, but her repentance is not true repentance ; and an extravagant Antinomian form of Protestantism also separates them, and preaches *faith* without even naming repentance—but this faith is not Bible faith at all. By repentance the sinner's heart is broken, by faith the broken heart is sweetly healed by Christ. The Holy Spirit works both, and works them simultaneously, and not one before the other.

We have got in our day into a miserable way of showing our faith by our *words;* and because our *words* are very good words, we account our faith to be well authenticated by them, as good and true. And we have got also into a way of comparing ourselves with ourselves, and with one another, and because we are not worse than our fellows—perhaps to appearance a little better—we are pretty well satisfied. It is not by our good *words*, but by our good *works*, that our faith is to be shown (James ii. 20–26). And we are to compare ourselves, not with each other, but with the only standard, the lofty requirements of God's most Holy Word. And this is illustrated for us in the example which Christ gave us in the life which He lived, in order to furnish us with a model. And the *works* which authenticate faith are not merely the common decencies and moralities of life—the negative goodness which consists in the absence of scandals; even heathen virtue, unbelieving virtue, infidel virtue can rise above this. Our works are to be works which NOTHING BUT FAITH can accomplish, and which are therefore infallible proofs that the man who works them is IN LIVING FELLOWSHIP with the living Christ. I do not mean to say that the FORM of the works done will always be extraordinary; no, the outward form will generally be very commonplace, but then these commonplace, ordinary works shall be performed in a very extraordinary spirit—a spirit that is Christ-like and unearthly.

And then, whatever we discover within us that

does not come up to the high level of God's holy requirements and our blessed Lord's perfect example, we should meet at once with a fresh act of repentance towards God, and faith towards our Lord Jesus Christ.

When one begins to think of this subject, its lengths and breadths are so immense that one knows not how to say *merely* a few words. Before saying a word further, I would like to premise two remarks. First, That repentance is not a certain feeling, or set of feelings, that we are called on to work up in our own hearts. Ah, no! of ourselves we cannot repent aright ; we can do nothing (John xv. 5). The repentance which comes from *me* merely, is like myself, selfish and sinful, and needs to be repented of. Christ GIVES repentance, as He gives forgiveness (Acts v. 31), and we accept both at His hands.

Second, We must never think of God as reluctant to meet the returning sinner with His overflowing love. God's love is HOLY LOVE, and His joyous readiness to meet and to welcome the returning sinner, even at the beginning of his return, is inconceivable (Luke xv. 20). There is no particle then of a *legal* feeling in the repentance of the New Testament.

Repentance is one grand theme of the Bible. Every Old Testament prophet, every one, calls to IT. The Baptist had for his main work to call to repentance; when imprisoned, the Lord Jesus took up his cry, and urged men to repent (Matt. iv. 17). When He sent out the twelve He summed up in two most comprehensive words the entire burden of this testimony (see Luke xxiv. 47). In the one word "REMISSION" He includes all the blessedness which is freely bestowed by God on man through Christ Jesus; in the word "REPENTANCE" He includes everything which on man's part constitutes a due response to God's call in the Gospel, and on these instructions the Apostles acted (see Peter, Acts ii. 37, 38; see Paul in the summary of his work, Acts xx. 21).

Nor is this repentance obsolete. Seven letters were dictated by our Lord after His ascension to heaven, and in these repentance is as urgently pressed as ever (see Rev. ii. 5, 16, and iii. 3, 19).

Perhaps we might try to glance at ONE invariable aspect of a true evangelical repentance, remembering that it is only one of the many forms in which a genuine repentance manifests itself. For this special form of repentance, as it works in the heart of every true penitent, read carefully Ezek. xvi. 63.

What a loathsome picture of sin, of all sin, as God sees it have we set before us under a similitude in the preceding parts of the chapter. It is overwhelming when we take it home. We see sin— our own sin—to be infinitely loathsome, and are filled with a hatred of it, and a humiliation because of it, that defy expression (1 TIM. i. 15 ; Job xlii. 6).

In spite of Israel's inconceivable wickedness, God remembered His *covenant* (verse 60). For His grace ABOUNDS even beyond men's sin (Rom. v. 20). This covenant is spoken of in verse 8. The sinner's only hope lies here. OUR covenant is in Christ.

When God remembers His covenant, she " remembers" her sin (verse 61). She had never done this in the depth of her wickedness, and this remembrance of her sins makes her *ashamed* (verse 61). In the days of her wickedness, so proud was she in her self-righteousness that she could not endure to name Sodom and Samaria (verses 56, 57). For the sinner, though he sees the sinfulness of others (in part), never sees his own utter loathsomeness. But Israel, now penitent, sees that she had been far worse than despised Sodom and Samaria, and is ashamed *of herself*, when they are given to her as her *daughters in grace.* For she now learns (verse 62) what God is, not through His holy judgments, but through His holy mercy.

And the result—the designed result of the whole —is that she is *confounded* (stronger than ashamed in verse 61). She was ashamed to be made superior in blessing (mother and daughters) to Sodom and Samaria. She who was really so much worse than Sodom—though she had fancied herself to be so much better (verses 48, 56)—but she is confounded when God goes on to add to her the infinite blessings of the NEW and BETTER covenant.

She cannot *"open her mouth"* in view of so much mercy (verse 63). Not one word of excuse— no penitent ever has. He has not even begun to repent who palliates his enormous wickedness (Rom. iii. 19). Not one word, but lowly confession and fervent praise.

And all this while enjoying to the full God's utmost favour. He is now "PACIFIED towards her;" and she has the joy of knowing it. Her sins are not only forgiven but forgotten (Heb. x. 17). But like every true penitent, she cannot forgive herself—her sin is "ever before" her (Ps. li. 3), not to distress or even disturb, but to deepen her adoring *joy* IN GOD. This is, I do believe, the characteristic attitude of a gracious soul towards the forgiving God, and towards the forgiven sin. Towards the one it turns with unutterable joy, and love, and trust, wondering at the riches of a grace that can deal with such a sinner ; from the other it turns away with shame and grief, confounded at its own wickedness, that it could so wantonly abuse the mercy of such a Father (2 COR. vii. 11).

Now, how rare comparatively is the combination of these two feelings. We have any number of professors who have peace, and who never doubt that God is pacified towards them ; but they have oh, how slight a consciousness of their enormous guiltiness ! They are not " CONFOUNDED " at the wonderful mercy that could forgive sinners like them—nay, they are not even " ASHAMED " when they look at themselves beside other forgiven ones, and remember that their forgiveness needed so much more grace than the forgiveness of others (1 Tim. i. 15). In fact, they are as self-ignorant and self-satisfied *as* THE CARELESS *round about them are,* as Israel was when in the depth of her wickedness she never suspected herself to be so wicked (verse 56). There are others, again, who are more or less convicted of exceeding sinfulness, but who little realise that God is pacified towards them for the sake of

Christ and His blood, who have too imperfectly learned what God really is—through the freeness and the greatness of His forgiving love towards themselves (Luke vii. 47). This is not the Christian's suitable frame of spirit ; nevertheless, I take it to be often unspeakably better than the former.

Oh, to be sunk down to the lowest, and every day to be sinking lower and still lower in self-con-founded, dumb-stricken self-abasement—while, *at the same time,* one is raised to the highest pitch of adoring gladness, in the joyous apprehension of that pardoning mercy which, *in Christ Jesus,* delights to heap its favours on the heads of such sinners. For me, I desire that God may work in me the utmost attainable measure of this penitence.

It is only when these two—the joy and the tender sorrow—are thus combined that either of them is safe for us. The joy alone, without the sorrow, is dangerous, for it tends to pride ; the sorrow alone is dangerous, for it comes out of unbelief, even so far as to despair ; but the two combined make us strong in the Lord. When thus *suitably* combined, there is not a particle of bitterness in our sorrow ; for we rejoice IN GOD as being perfectly pacified towards us; while there is not a particle of self-elevation in our joy, since we are *confounded*, stricken dumb in view of a mercy that has pardoned EVEN ME. And it is to produce this very blending of the two feelings that God trains us as He does. When He fills the swelling heart full with the joy of His salvation, He never fails to reveal at the same time more of that heart's own vileness; otherwise we would take the glory of it all to ourselves, and would poison ourselves with our very blessedness. At the same time, He never reveals to us our own enormity (in our fleshly selves), except very gradually; for if we were to see it all at once, so great is it, and so appalling would the vision be, that we should be overpowered by sheer despair. But bit by bit, He opens up to us more and more of His fulness of grace and glory in Christ Jesus, and more and more of our own unworthiness; and so we are neither puffed up by the one, nor crushed by the other ; but, walking with Himself in joyous love, are more and more confounded at the growing vision of His *unbounded goodness* and of *our own depravity.*

It is this too that makes Christ so precious to penitent souls. Nothing in heaven or on earth is so precious as Christ is, to one who has been thus humbled. And nothing is so little cared for as the

2:5

actual Christ is, by a self-confident unhumbled
professor. His joy is in his OWN FAITH, or some
one or other of his own exercises; but he never
rejoices *purely and simply* as a naked sinner, as
nothing else but only a sinner—FRANKLY FORGIVEN
all for Christ's sake only.

The Holy Spirit's first work on every soul is one
of conviction (John xvi. 9). But, as hinted above,
this first work of conviction is incomplete, and
needs to be carried on from one stage to another.
It is deep enough in the sinner's case to answer the
end designed, which end is to bring him off from
all self-confidence to trust in Christ. And now
when the man becomes a saint, the Holy Spirit
carries on His work in the soul and reveals CHRIST,
and SELF, to the man in ever-growing clearness.
And when He does so, we ought never to protect
ourselves from the deep wounds which the Holy
Spirit gives to our carnal self-sufficiency by our
misuse of Gospel truth. The Gospel never was
meant to be used in this way. The Gospel itself,
when received, delivers us from the curse of the
broken law, but the faith of it never was meant to
deliver us from the *shame* and the *grief* (holy and
gracious grief) of having wantonly and wickedly
broken that law. Nay, rather, if I receive God's

wonderful mercy in a proper spirit, I shall use my deepening sense of it to aggravate my sin, but never to excuse it. Shall I think myself less vile because God's goodness is so amazing? The Gospel is meant, as it is fitted, sweetly to comfort us—but it is to comfort us AS HUMBLE, not to comfort us *as* proud. " Blessed are they that *mourn;* for THEY shall be comforted " (Matt. v. 4).

The passover supper (Exod. xii.) needed the roasted lamb, which typified Christ crucified ; but the roasted flesh was to be eaten along *with bitter herbs*, which (I believe) symbolised the very penitence we are speaking of. And just as it could be no passover without the lamb, so neither could it be a passover without the bitter herbs, and the unleavened bread which symbolised perfect sincerity (1 Cor. v. 8).

But the subject is well-nigh endless ; may the Lord teach us more and more about these gracious experiences in the fullest enjoyment of them. Grace, grace, infinite, free, sovereign grace—this alone can meet the need of fallen man. Let me simply add with awe, that the tendency to abuse this grace, and thus to destroy himself by his abuse of it, is about the strongest tendency in the human heart. And in our day this all but irresistible tendency is not sufficiently guarded against.

The above is only a single aspect of a subject which has many aspects.

CHAPTER V.

LIVING BY FAITH.

WE allow ourselves to reason far too much—
I am speaking only of our treatment of
spiritual matters—while we trust in God with
entire singleness of heart far too little. The
injury which is done to ourselves in this way no
tongue could tell. Our entire blessedness as men
"in Christ," comes to us only as we exercise this
simple faith; while such faith finds no enemies so
powerful as these same fleshly reasonings. They
exalt themselves against our due acknowledgment
of God (2 Cor. x. 5), and we shall make little
progress until, with the promised help of God, we
cast them down. As *Christians* we are called to
walk by faith, amid circumstances where all *others*
walk by sight (2 Cor. v. 7). Every act which is
not done by us in faith is, as a consequence, done
in sin (Rom. xiv. 23). Of course, to walk by faith

implies that we do not see our own way; but
that, trusting in Him who sees it perfectly, we
commit ourselves to His gracious guidance. In
this way, faith has always to be exercised *in the
dark.* But since God is what we believe Him to
be — infinite in every adorable perfection—how
safely may we trust Him! At the same time, and
just because He is thus infinite in His perfections,
our trust must necessarily be trust *in the dark*—
trust IN HIMSELF without any adequate comprehension of His plans on our part. How could we be
able to grasp with intelligence the immense reaches
of His stupendous purposes of love? Be it enough
for us that we are warranted to exclaim with joy,
whatever our outward lot may be: "I am poor
and needy, but the Lord is planning for me" (Ps.
xl. 17).

Indeed, in receiving Christ, as the Father gives
Him to us, we disown for ever all trust in
our own wisdom. This thought is less familiar to
us than another thought is—that, in order to a
man's being found in Christ and having His righteousness, the man needs to cast away and to disown
his own. It is not until the man sees his own
righteousness to be but filthy rags, to be nothing but
loss, that he can find true rest of heart in "THE

LORD OUR RIGHTEOUSNESS" (Jer. xxiii. 6). And
the case is the same in regard to Christ as our
wisdom. He is made of God to us our exclusive
wisdom, as He is made our exclusive righteousness
(1 Cor. i. 30). Apart from Him we have no true
wisdom or righteousness; and to enjoy Him as
actually our wisdom and our righteousness, we need
absolutely to reject our own. How grievously
then do we sin, and how sadly do we suffer, when
we allow ourselves to lean to our own understanding instead of trusting in the Lord with all our
hearts (Prov. iii. 5).

And I do think that there is no subject of
spiritual interest concerning which we are more
ready to indulge these fleshly reasonings, or where
they are more full of mischief to ourselves, than
when we attempt to judge the varied bearings of
our own earthly lot. Unlike that of the Lord Jesus,
judgment is after the " sight of our eyes " (Isa. xi.
3). We forget that it is utterly impossible for the
fleshly mind to estimate aright the things of the
spirit (1 Cor. ii. 11–14), as impossible as it is for
the cattle in the fields, or the dogs in the streets.
And though the Christian is not now, as he once
was, led by his fleshly mind, that mind is still in
him, to be a cause of constant conflict and a source

of perpetual danger. And the carnal mind is, in
the believer, just what it is in the unbeliever—
" Enmity against God," not subject to God, and
incapable of subjection (Rom. viii. 7).   The Christian, therefore, has to mortify it daily ; and in so far
as he fails to do this, his spirit is carnal and his
walk shall be unsteady. If, by its very wisdom,
the world is kept in ignorance of God (1 Cor. i. 21)
the Christian too, by the same fleshly wisdom, so
far as he follows it, is kept in partial ignorance
and in grievous weakness.

We see what a muddle Job and his friends got
into when they attempted to solve Job's case by
their own reasonings about it. At the close God
graciously interposed to correct their mistakes ; but
how did He do so ? Was it by pointing out to
them some flaw in their logic, by explaining to
them the details of His methods and His plans ?
It was anything but this. He gave no countenance whatever to their presumptuous reasonings
on such subjects ; but He simply recalled to Job
the grand truth which they had all forgotten, that
God's majesty is infinitely above man's conception
of it, and that His ways of wisdom are altogether
beyond man's power to trace. He brought them
to the self-abased submission of simple, unreasoning

trust ; and they reached rest, not in *seeing* but in believing. Let us with our whole hearts come to Job's final finding as soon as possible ; and, abhorring ourselves for our indulgence of this carnal self-reliant wisdom in the past, let us repent of it in dust and ashes. " I hate thoughts," cries the Psalmist, " but Thy law do I love " (Ps. cxix. 113).

We sometimes say to the perplexed sinner, in the words of the hymn—

> " All is finished ! do not doubt it,
> But believe thy dying Lord ;
> Never reason more about it,
> Only take Him at His word."

Might we not say the same thing to ourselves ofttimes when depressed and perplexed ? Just as bodily pain is proof of disease somewhere, so spiritual perplexity is proof of defective faith. And just as the troubled sinner needs simple faith to put him into possession of Christ, so the troubled saint needs simple faith to bring him into a fuller enjoyment of the unsearchable riches of Christ. We see from Old Testament prophecy, and from our Lord's own sayings, that God the Father had a minutely detailed life-plan for His beloved Son. He has a life-plan for every child of His, equally minute. Oh, if His special providence includes in its care the chattering sparrow, can it overlook the blood-redeemed child? And if it take note of the hairs of his head, shall it neglect the weightiest of all his interests? Let us cast all our burdens on the Lord, and *see that we leave them with Him,* seeking grace to say continually, as our Lord said, " I have come not to do my own will but the will of Him that sent me."

Oh, my brother, what amazing grace it is that the Son of God condescended to die on the Cross for our guilt ; and, also, that in equal condescension of love He stoops now to live in us, and through us, so filling up the details of our earthly lives that the living is both HIS and OURS (Gal. ii. 20). May He help me—dust and ashes—to aim at this point ceaselessly, that I walk worthy of Him (Col. i. 10). Oh, it is inexpressibly sweet to cast one's burden on the Lord, as He bids us do, and TO LEAVE IT WITH HIM ; to say with the joyous whole-heartedness of child-like faith, " HE DOETH ALL THINGS WELL." Therefore, whatever God is graciously pleased to appoint for us WILL BE OUR MOST HEARTY CHOICE. His power can never fail, His love cannot fail, His wisdom cannot mistake ; what a matchless blessing, then, to have all our concerns at the disposal of our

FATHER—infinite in His love, His wisdom, and His power !

There is abundant rest in Christ our Lord for all sorely burdened and weary ones; but such is the strange opposition, both from within us and without us, to our entering into this incomparable rest, that we need to LABOUR in order to enter in (Heb. iv. 11).

God gives everything to faith, and we are so utterly poor, that He has also to give us the faith which enables us to receive, as well as the blessing which faith receives. The faith which He gives we are to use under the Holy Spirit's direction and help. It is we ourselves must believe, for God will never believe in our room. He is giving us ample grounds for our faith, and every help to believing that we can need, but it is we, ourselves, who must believe. How sad that our alienation from God is so complete that we find it so hard and difficult to trust Him, and have so often to cry to Him in sorrow, " Lord, I believe, help Thou mine unbelief."

With what a spirit of free, unhindered liberty may the Christian, walking in communion with his Father, pass through this life. As the free-man of Christ he is free indeed; and no created power can

put any constraint upon Him. He may be outwardly a slave, really, he is more free than his
master; he may be as poor as Lazarus, he is, in
truth, richer than any king. For HE CHOOSES
WITH ALL HIS HEART to be the very slave or pauper
that he is, seeing that GOD has appointed this to
be his condition. He desires the WHOLE WILL OF
GOD; and he finds all his delight, either in doing
it or in bearing it. Let the man CHOOSE what
his Father hath already CHOSEN FOR HIM,
and the very blessedness of Heaven will follow such
living by faith—the "My peace" of the Lord
Jesus (John xiv. 27) shall enter at once into his
heart.

CHAPTER VI.

THE PRODIGAL'S RETURN.

I HAVE been musing on that wonderful chapter, Luke xv. Perhaps there is no portion of Holy Scripture which I read so often. It is the story of my own life. I am the lost sheep, and the dropped coin, and the most foolish and wicked son. It was to seek for me that the Shepherd came, and the woman lighted her candle and took her broom; and it was to welcome me that the rejoicing Father made His feast. What a wonderful difference it makes when, in reading God's words, we apply every one of them to ourselves, feeling that He is not only speaking them TO ME, but speaking them, in some way or other, ABOUT MYSELF.

I am touched inexpressibly by one feature which is brought out clearly in all the three parables : the exuberant joy with which the recovery of a sinner is welcomed (see verses 7, 10, 20 to 24).

How it touches our hearts to take this home to
ourselves ; to think that GOD, and Christ, and all
the holy beings in heaven, should be thrilled with
raptures of joy over worms like you and ME.   It
can be no paltry interest which is able to awaken
such deep emotion.   And yet this event, which in
heaven is counted so stupendous, is counted
nothing at all on earth.   What a grand thing,
then, must a GENUINE conversion be when it
gives such joy to GOD, and sends a wave of holy
gladness over the measureless breadths of heaven !
And what a view does this give us of the unselfish
love of all holy creatures, and, still more, of the
love of God, of whose love the love of all creatures
is but a tiny droplet !

And are we among the holy, who rejoice with
exultant joy over every sinner's recovery that we
become cognisant of ; or, what is much the same
thing, are we sorrowing over the hardness of human
hearts, which persist in rejecting the Divine mercy,
and, though called, will not return ?   And are we,
in persevering prayer for such, pouring out our
hearts before God in groanings which cannot be
uttered ?

And let us notice that all this is for ONE SOUL,
for ANY one, for EVERY returning one — for

YOU, or for ME. Heaven the holy, Heaven the
happy, is made happier by the return of every
repenting sinner, and see from verses 20 to 24 how
God rejoices in having found the lost object of His
LOVE. So entirely different from all this is the state
of feeling upon earth, that men not only do not
rejoice over a conversion, but, in general, cannot be
stirred up to take any interest in the salvation of
THEMSELVES.

And who among us, beloved brother, has not
needed to return to God in humble broken hearted
penitence, OFTENER THAN ONCE? If there
be any who have not fallen back, and needed
restoration, I am not one of them. Blessed be
God that His wonderful love is such, that He can
receive and welcome back to His bosom EVEN
BACKSLIDERS; He not only pardons, but He
MULTIPLIES to pardon (Isa. lv. 7, margin).
This is surely greater grace than to receive any
sinner at first. But many have found it more
difficult to return than when they came to the
Saviour at first. God abhors backsliding, and so
He teaches His children, through painful experi-
ences, to abhor, and dread, and watch against it.

But let it never be lost sight of that Jesus
receives all who come to Him as sinners, desiring

salvation from His gracious hands——He refuses none, NOT EVEN A BACKSLIDER. Only such a man must come as he came at first, AS A SINNER AND NOTHING ELSE, yea, come more deeply humbled than he was at first, for his sin is so very much greater, and if he be truly penitent, he will do so ; and GOD, unchangeably the same, shall receive him with the same tenderness of forgiving love, which shall be to the backslider's eyes more wonderful and sweeter than even his first experience of it.

What an astonishing word is that in Rom. v. 20 : "Where SIN abounded GRACE (OUR SIN and GOD'S GRACE) did much more abound." Can anything be conceived as greater than the enormous guilt of any and every sinner ? Yes, for the grace of God is INFINITELY GREATER; the mercy which pardons the guilt, and the grace which brings every needed help to overcome. The only reason, then, why any soul remains unblest is simply this : "YE WILL NOT come unto Me" (John v. 40). Why cannot, or why does not, the sinner believe ? Because he WILL not. And why cannot, why does not, the saint live in the daily or hourly accomplishment of what to nature are impossibilities ? Chiefly because he WILL not. "I WOULD, but ye would not," accounts often for failure in regard to spiritual things. So far as God is concerned, there is no hindrance to the Christ-likeness of ANY believer, if only the man put himself into his Saviour's hands to be made perfectly Christ-like, COST WHAT IT WILL.

All this is quite familiar to each of us; but the battle is to reduce the whole to daily practice, to walk continually in the full power of it. And this, too, the Lord is willing, is waiting, to give. We are all wants and emptiness, but He is all FULNESS; and He would have us bring our emptiness to Him, that He may have the ceaseless joy of filling our emptiness out of His fulness; and we, the ceaseless joy of being so filled by one whom we so love.

I can easily fancy some one saying in astonished bewilderment: "I cannot understand all this exuberance of grace; I know not how to think of it." No, indeed, you cannot understand it. Its IMMENSITY puts it above the comprehension of angels as well as of men. The breadths and the lengths, the depths and the heights, of the love of Christ passeth knowledge. Let us not expect to understand it; let us do what is infinitely better —let us appropriate it, let us make it all our very surest OWN; and then let us go on to enjoy it up to our uttermost capacity for enjoying anything.

2:6

CHAPTER VII.

I WILL IN NO WISE CAST OUT.

WE shall try to gather up hastily the story of a saved soul, as we have it in this Scripture (John vi. 37–45) set before us. It begins first with God. The process begins by the Father's giving the soul that is to be saved to the Son, in order that the Son may save it (see verse 37). But this transaction is secret between the Father and the Son. Note, as the second stage, that the Father goes on to TEACH the soul whom He has given to His Son (see verse 45). For, though the man may have been perfectly familiar with the outward letter of Gospel truth, he has been sitting inwardly in darkness and the shadow of death. Dr. Chalmers had been a minister for years before he was taught of God, and there are many preachers who live and die untaught. The lessons which God, at first, teaches the soul are mainly these

two : Its own awful wickedness and utter helplessness to make itself any better; along with this,
He reveals to its wondering vision the love and the
loveliness of the Lord Jesus ; and how able, how
ready, how delighted He is to save TO THE
UTTERMOST every coming sinner.

The third stage is, that, by means of this teaching, the Father DRAWS the soul toward Christ
(see verse 44). The man, seeing clearly and feel-
ingly what a ruined and sinful creature he is, and
seeing as clearly the fitness of Christ as a Saviour
for such a lost sinner, is sweetly drawn to desire,
with growing vehemence, a share in this salvation
which Christ has come to bring. And the more he
looks at self in all its horror and loathsomeness,
and at Christ in all His attractive grace and glory
—the more he feels it impossible to remain any
longer where he still is — a wretched sinner,
who is justly CONDEMNED ALREADY, and this
to eternal death (John iii. 18).

Now comes the fourth stage. The man thus
drawn Christwards through the Father's teaching,
now yields to the powerful drawing which he feels
in his heart, and so he actually comes to Christ AS
A SINNER, in order that Christ AS THE SAVIOUR
may save him (see verse 37). The drawing is

very powerful, but it never does any violence to
the perfect freedom of the man's own choice. He
comes MOST WILLINGLY, and yet, knowing
what the Father has taught him, HE CANNOT BUT
COME.

Then instantly follows the fifth stage (verse 37).
The sinner thus coming to Christ is ALWAYS and
MOST HEARTILY WELCOMED BY HIM. He in no
wise shall cast out ANY coming one. It is
utterly IMPOSSIBLE that He should. He receives
the sinner with a joy that is inconceivable. Read
how He speaks of this joy in Luke xv. 5, 6, 7, 10,
20–24. He sees in the sinner's actual coming to
Him the fact that the Father has been teaching
and drawing the soul, and that it is the Father's
WILL that He should save THAT SOUL. And so He
welcomes the coming sinner with greatest delight
of love, for He came simply to DO THE FATHER'S
WILL ; and He sees and knows that it is *the*
FATHER'S WILL THAT He should save it, and should
raise it up in final glory at the last day (see verse
39. And He saves the soul, not merely because of
His own great love to sinful men, but also as an
act of obedience to His Father's will.

We shall not follow out the process any further,
but shall sum up all that follows the welcoming of

the sinner into one stage, which we may count the sixth. Jesus takes such a strong and loving hold of the soul which the Father has given Him to save, that He shall never, NEVER relax His grip ; but in the words of Jude 24, " Shall present it faultless before the face of the Father's glory, with exceeding joy." Of all whom He has thus undertaken to His Father to save, He has lost none ; NO, NOT A SINGLE ONE (verse 39). Oh, let us see that we trust Him UTTERLY.

Of course God never brings any two souls to glory in exactly the same way ; there are always differences, greater or less. But there are the same broad and general features in all cases, and I venture to think that these are in a cursory way stated in our little sketch. Let it never be forgotten, however, that no certain amount of conviction is needed before Christ will accept a coming sinner. The degree of conviction is needed, not to induce Christ to welcome us, but to *constrain* US TO COME to Him. Some gentle souls are drawn by a very little of it ; others who are harder need almost the flashings of God's thunderbolts. But the welcome is all the same, IF ONLY THE SINNER COMES. And if a man has had conviction enough to constrain him to flee to the

Saviour, he has quite enough for his present need.

It would help many a Christian from being needlessly dejected to recognise the fact that, in one sense, salvation is a PROCESS; as such it is carried onward towards completion *through many stages*. Regeneration, which gives life to the soul dead in sins, is always instantaneous, though it may have needed much preparation ere the soul was fitted to receive it. But then, REGENERATION by itself is not SALVATION in its FULL and COMPLETE sense, but only the first part of it. Salvation includes sanctification, and that is a life-long process. Therefore Paul calls on those already entered on the path of salvation to work out their own salvation with fear and trembling (Phil. ii. 12, 13). And as for himself, the apostle took his own advice, for he felt that he had not yet attained that for the attainment of which Christ had laid hold on him, and so, forgetting the past, he pressed on, and on, and on, with ever-growing eagerness, to reach heights which hitherto he had never reached.

Now, all this is both a joyful and often a sorrowful experience. It is sorrowful because in the course of it the holy soul gets opened up before its eyes depths of its own sinfulness, which it had not suspected, in order that it may be still further driven out from all trust in self, and may cling with more entire singleness of heart to Jesus only; and these discoveries are very painful, as well as very humbling, to the child of God; but they always lead to increase of joy. He is thereby sent, day after day, to Christ afresh, who becomes to him more and more all his salvation and all his desire. Thus are we trained to walk by FAITH, and to find our EVERYTHING in Christ.

CHAPTER VIII.

SALVATION—WHAT IS IT?

FREE Salvation seems in these days to be confounded by not a few with easy salvation. God be thanked for making salvation *so* PERFECTLY FREE, for how otherwise could it ever be attained by creatures like us, "DEAD in trespasses and sins"? But we shall mistake the whole matter if we think of God's salvation as being easy because it is free. Nothing, indeed, is so easily to be got, since the God who "delighteth in mercy" refuses it to no coming seeker; but at the same time, nothing is so hard, as truly, in the fullest sense, to take and enjoy as this great salvation, since the enjoyment of it involves the sacrifice of that which man, as fallen and therefore rebellious, cares to possess. But He who accomplished the mighty work for sinners on the Cross, is now carrying it forward to completion on the Throne; and though we cannot trace His workings, He is really administering His universal providence over earth, in the highest interests of His own Kingdom and people.

How very encouraging, but how very sifting, are the holy words which the apostle uses when speaking of this " SALVATION," free and full, which God has provided for ALL ! (Titus ii. 11). At what a cost has it been provided ; the Son of God had to " GIVE HIMSELF " for us (verse 14). How freely and how readily it is bestowed upon the chief of sinners we see hinted at here, and more clearly brought out in such passages as Luke xv. But what really constitutes the actual salvation, which Christ did not grudge the sacrifice of Himself to procure ? He did it all in order that " He might *redeem* US from ALL INIQUITY, and purify *unto Himself* a peculiar people, ZEALOUS of GOOD WORKS." This was Christ's end in dying—this is what He means by SALVATION. Hence the Gospel word that brings us this salvation " teaches us that, denying ungodliness and worldly lusts, we should live soberly, righteously, and godly in this present world, looking for that blessed hope, and the glorious appearing of the great God and our Saviour Jesus Christ."

Is this what is commonly understood by " SAL-

VATION"? I know it is by some, but is it not
sometimes limited to a deliverance merely from the
wrath to come? Of course, Christ does this too;
but Christ's end was to "save His people FROM
THEIR SINS" (Matt. i. 21), and he that is not, in the
prevailing tenor of his spirit, saved from the sin in
which he once lay dead (Eph. ii. 1), shall find to
his dismay at last that neither is he saved from
hell. And at what a pitch of holy devotedness the
saved man is expected to live! Every such man is
to be, in every respect, a PATTERN saint (Titus ii. 7).
Nay, to rise higher still, if it be possible, his life is
to be an ORNAMENT, and an ornament in ALL
respects, to Bible doctrine (Titus ii. 10). But how can
man ever rise up to this pitch? it may be asked.
Of course of himself, DEAD IN SIN, he can do nothing
acceptable; but the believing man is not left to
himself (see Gal. ii. 20). So far from this, he is
"THOROUGHLY FURNISHED" for such holy living
by the inspired Word for his guide (2 Tim. iii. 16),
and by the Almighty Spirit as his efficient power
(Phil. iv. 13); and so, while without Christ we can
do nothing (John xv. 5), in Him, we can do what
God calls us to. And the uniform tenor of Holy
Scripture (the New Testament) is the same. Is
Christ our head? then we are called on, and

strengthened (if we accept the help) for walk that
is to be "WORTHY" of Christ, in ALL respects
being universally fruitful (see Col. i. 10). Oh,
my brother, it lays me on my face in the dust, when
I think of laying my poor, spotted, unsteady life (as
a Christian) beside His, and looking at the two
together, and I dare not even ask the question, Is
my life WORTHY, WORTHY, WORTHY of Him?
Yet He bids me to make it so, expects it, and has
"thoroughly furnished" me for it.

And similarly, we are to walk worthy (worthy
again) of God, as our Father, and of the glory to
which, as our Father, He has called us (1 Thess. ii.
12). His own fervent faith lifted up the apostle into
this lofty region (see verse 10); and he tells them
(verse 13) that when received aright the mighty
Word of God "*effectually* worketh also" in the same
way in them that believe. Similarly we are called
on to walk "worthy" of our vocation (Eph. iv. 1),
which wonderful vocation is set before us in a light
positively overpowering in chapters i., ii., iii. Yet
we are to walk WORTHY of it.

Oh, my brother, how one-sided is the preaching of
the Gospel of the day we are now living in! There
is nothing which men so love to hear as "Peace
peace," whether there be solid grounds for peace or

no.   They are all ear on this side of the head, but
on the other side—the side at which God is speaking of His claims, and telling that the life in Christ
is to be enjoyed only as we die to self, and that this
is God's great purpose in saving us—men are deaf
enough.   And at the same time there is nothing
so easy or so pleasant as to preach the same Peace,
peace, and to get poor sinners to believe it.   It is
getting to be popular doctrine.   It is also the
highway to great success in preaching, as things
are too often judged.   Our sole path of safety lies
in our being led step by step by that most holy
and most loving Lord, who is able to KEEP that
which we commit to Him (2 Tim. i. 12), and
who will guide His own (so committed) through
wiles and false snares and misleading attractions,
which are so cunningly set forth that *if it were
possible*, IF IT WERE POSSIBLE, they would deceive
the VERY elect (Matt. xxiv. 24).   And you and I and
all, who would fain bring before others the Gospel
word, have a double responsibility.   We are weighted
as it were with the weight of other souls besides our
own—those, namely, who give heed to us.   Often
does the word in Heb. xiii. 17, come up on my
mind, " They watch for souls; as they that must give
account."   Here is sloth rebuked—they " WATCH

for souls ; " and here, too, is fleshly zeal and self-
willed rashness rebuked——" as they who must give
account."

Those who preach the Gospel should use God's
revealed truth about the Lord Jesus Christ, to
enlighten the *understanding,* and through that to
rouse the *conscience,* to engage the affections, and
to decide THE WILL ; and when this is done a
soul is really helped ; but merely to excite the
EMOTIONS, especially by some vulgar appeals, and
then tell the person with the excited feeling that
he or she is now converted, is sadly unscriptural,
and may be fatally misleading.   May the Lord
keep us sincere, and without offence, until the day
of Christ.

CHAPTER IX.

THE HEART.

1. A COLD HEART.

I AM very happy to hear you moaning over the coldness of your heart, and expressing strong desire for more warmth of love to the Lord Jesus.

And He Himself has put this SENSE of coldness in your heart, and this yearning for a warmer love; just that you may go to Him to get it, for He wants you to have it in the fullest measure. You never knew a tender love which did not yearn with vehement desire for the love of the beloved one in return; and it is so with the wonderful love of Christ to ourselves. Our coldness to Him grieves His Spirit, while such is the fervour of His love to us, that He cannot rest contented without our full-hearted love in return. "My Son," He says, "GIVE Me THINE HEART" (Prov. xxiii. 26).

How perfectly certain is it, then, that He is

ready to bestow on us this matchless blessing of a
warm, loving heart, if only we be ready to receive
it. We can count on HIS readiness ALWAYS.
LOVE is the first, and also the most precious, of the
fruits of the SPIRIT (Gal. v. 22), which Spirit, along
with His fruits, is given in answer to prayer ; and
how infinitely ready our most loving Father is to
give us the Holy Spirit with all His fruits we may
see in the astonishing assurance given us in
Luke xi. 13. But, in addition to prayer for it,
a great help to increase of love will be found in
devout meditation on two things—the LOVE of
Jesus, and the LOVELINESS of Jesus. Suppose
we sit down and give ourselves up to muse on
Christ's LOVE to us, and also on the LOVELINESS
of His matchless character, as you find them in the
four Gospels ; and as we see, and feel, in regard to
the wonderful glories of Him who is, to all who
really know Him, " the altogether LOVELY," perhaps, thus musing, the Divine fire may burn in our
hearts, and we shall not be left long to mourn the
absence of love.

I would like, however, to say that frequently
the first beginning of a true response from our
hearts, in return for the great and free love of God
to us, does not take the form of a warm and lively

love to Him on our part ; but simply of a distressing consciousness, that our hearts have been so
hard, and so cold hitherto, that they have not been
melted as they should by the great love of God
to us.   And this thought, in connection with
thoughts of God's love to us, humbles, grieves,
alarms, and convinces us that we must be very
vile and sinful creatures indeed !   Notice carefully
what it is which thus convicts us of sin, and
which humbles, grieves, distresses, and alarms us.
It is not the law of God, with its threatenings and
its terrors ; it is not any selfish dread of sufferings
or of punishment in another world.   It is the soft,
gentle, sweetly-melting pleadings of the love of
God, lovingly speaking within our hearts, and
which makes us upbraid ourselves with deep sorrow
and shame that we have so wickedly neglected it.

But the same gentle love which is wounding us
in this way, is also healing us ; it is killing us only
to make us alive ; it is making us to feel painfully
how empty we are, that it may make us desire
eagerly, and welcome heartily, the provided filling.
For what is this Divine love saying to us when it
awakens this grief in us ?   It speaks thus : My
poor, miserable, but none the less My tenderly
beloved one, you are thus utterly wretched because

of your sin ; and your sin and your misery grieve
Me at My heart. And both your sin and its
consequent misery come out of the sad fact that
you do not love Me, though I so tenderly love you.
You CANNOT be happy or holy unless you love Me ;
and you never will be aught but a deep grief to
Me (such is My love to you), UNLESS YOU LOVE ME.
And then, when you give Me your heart, YOU AND
I shall rejoice in each other—I, in My long-lost,
but now happily recovered child ; and you, in your
long-forsaken, but now recovered Father. And
this call of God on us for love to Him is an offer
of Divine help, to enable us to render it, if we
avail ourselves of it ; nay, it involves a PROMISE
that He will bestow this love on us if we will
accept the precious gift. But notice that the
whole process begins in the belief that God so
tenderly loves us, while we, on our part, are conscious of failing to render Him our love in return.
Out of this grief and shame, that we love God so
feebly, grows a strong desire for adequate love to
Him ; and when a soul has been brought to this
first stage, all the rest will follow, step by step, if
the soul be in earnest about it.

The way to heaven lies always down through
the depths of humiliation. On the broken-hearted

2:7

penitent who groans out, God be merciful to me the sinner, for I have no goodness, no truth, no holiness, no happiness—on this man God smiles with favour at his self-abasing confession. He says to such humble penitents : NAY, thou art not ALL falseness, for thou hast spoken the truth about thyself just now. Neither is it true that there is nothing in thee but all unholiness and sin, for I AM IN THEE; and it is the light of My presence that is making thee see so clearly the depths of thine own wickedness. For My chosen abode is the humble and contrite heart (Isa. lvii. 15), and thy heart is such. But to the self-satisfied religious ones, who think themselves to be rich, and increased in goods, and needing nothing, He indignantly says that He will spue them out of His mouth with loathing. For the sure way to the heavenly heights lies for us through the deep depths of self-abasement; and one of the roads down to the depths of shame and everlasting contempt, is to climb the highest heights of our own self-righteousness. "For to this man will I look, saith the Lord, even to him that is poor and of a contrite spirit, and that trembleth at My Word" (Isa. lxvi. 2). And three times over the Lord repeats the solemn words : "Every one that *exalteth* himself shall be ABASED ; and he that HUMBLETH himself shall be exalted " (Luke xviii. 14).

---

2. A HARD HEART.

YOU speak of being troubled with a hard heart. And I rejoice, not in hearing that your heart is hard, but in thinking that God is teaching you, and that you are accepting His teaching. This is one of the most precious lessons which God our Father sets Himself to teach us ; and so reluctant are we to be taught the deeply humbling truth, that it takes a long time before we make much progress in the lesson. But He is a patient Teacher, and, as this lesson MUST BE TAUGHT us, He keeps us at it. At first, when we begin to be troubled about our sins, it is the remembrance of certain evil deeds, immoralities in speech or conduct, which distress us ; but in proportion as the Divine light reveals to us what *we are*, it is not so much these things which distress us, but the conscious-ness that WE ARE NOT what we ought to be.

Oh, then, let us be thankful even to tears of gratitude, when God is opening up to us the vision of our own evil heart. For it is He who is showing to us OUR HIDEOUS SELVES. We must not ascribe the making of these discoveries in ourselves to the working of our own mind. They are the workings of God's Holy Spirit in our soul. The natural man may indeed see and condemn such things as lying and stealing, brawling and drinking; but he never deplores the wickedness of a hard heart, for he does not see the essential wickedness of himself.

On the other hand, the Christian who is learning this precious lesson, is for a time more distressed than humbled by what he is seeing in himself, but, as he grows in grace and the knowledge of Christ, he comes to see a thousand times more evil in himself; and this shall more deeply HUMBLE him. It shall empty him the more perfectly of all confidence in the flesh (that is in himself), and cast him more absolutely on JESUS ONLY. Let you and me then encourage our hearts by remembering that, though our present convictions and humiliations be only like the feeble dawn, in which there is far more of darkness than of light, still it is the same sun which at the beginning of the day makes the dawn, that, at the middle of the day, makes the brilliant noon. In other words, it is the same GOD, acting in the same love, who, at this moment, is convincing us of our sin and misery, that wrought in Paul and John their seraph-like fervour ? Let us then fearlessly commit ourselves into His hands that He, who is already kindling the feeble day-dawn in our souls, may carry on His work in us, till it reach the blazing noon-day. And even then we may see more evil in ourselves than we do now; not that there shall be more evil in us to be seen, but more light to see it. I am delighted with the word of Paul when he was just about his holiest and his best, a prisoner at Rome, and waiting for the martyr's crown : " Unto me, who AM LESS THAN THE LEAST OF ALL SAINTS," &c. (Eph. iii. 8).

God aims at bringing us to see ourselves as we really are, void of all good, and filled with every evil. By nature we love the darkness rather than the light ; and He would have us know this (John iii. 19). We are sold UNDER SIN (Rom. vii. 14). By nature EVERY imagination of the thought of our heart is ONLY EVIL CONTINUALLY (Gen. vi. 5). When God speaks truth to us we don't believe it (John viii. 45); and when He offers good to us, we reject it. How true are His words : " O Israel, thou hast DESTROYED thyself; but IN ME is thy help " (Hosea xiii. 9). And since we need to be fully convinced of all this, it is in tender mercy that He shows us how lost we are, in order that we may cast our case with confidence upon His FULL, FREE love to us in Christ Jesus.

But though we must have a most humbling sense of our extreme sinfulness by nature, there is no need that this sense of sin should continue to distress and pain us. God means us to get rid of this distress, but we must see that we get rid of it only IN THE RIGHT WAY. It is like the burden on Christian's back in the " Pilgrim's Progress." Some pretenders professed to relieve pilgrims from their burdens in ruinous ways ; but Christian escaped from these, and his burden tumbled off of itself when he came to the Cross and the sepulchre. And so shall it be with us if we leave ourselves to God's leading. The burdensome sense of unspeakable vileness is given us that it may KILL us to our desperately tenacious self-righteousness, and help us to rest in SELF-EMPTIED faith on Jesus ONLY. When we do this, the DISTRESS is gone at once, though the HUMILITY grows greater and greater. Let us put our pride to death ; and then joy unspeakable shall spring up in our hearts, only it shall be ALTOGETHER JOY

IN THE LORD; and we shall then be no more distressed by the thought that we are infinitely indebted to the free mercy of God in Christ, than we are distressed to think that we are dependent on His almighty power to keep us alive.

----

3. A DECEITFUL HEART.

"THE heart is deceitful above all things, and desperately wicked," &c. (Jer. xvii. 9). This was the first Scripture that laid a strong hold of me in my youth; and it has tightened its grip on me year by year ever since. To a great extent it has given shape to my whole life, and I can see many a snare from which it has kept me. With tears of gratitude I thank my God for so pressing on me this truth. Shall we merely glance at it a little?

The verse connects with the preceding verses— Cursed is the man who trusts in man, and blessed alone is he who trusts in God. Now, we are just as ready to trust in man, especially in ourselves, as we are slow to trust in God; and while this is the case our blessing is impossible. And therefore it is that God tells us in verses 5 and 9 what we and our fellows all are, utterly unworthy of any trust. Our hearts are made up of two qualities, WICKEDNESS and DECEITFULNESS. For wickedness, they are DESPERATELY wicked; that is, all hope of finding them anything else than wicked is clean out of the question. For deceitfulness, they are deceitful above all things; they have no match in the universe of God. This being God's description of universal man, is not he who trusts either in his own heart, or in that of any other, a FOOL? (see Prov. xxviii. 26). In studying our own sinfulness, we should be more familiar with this solemn subject than with any other, except ONE. That one is the FULL, FREE LOVE of God to sinful YOU and ME, in Christ Jesus. Yes, study our sins; but never do this alone and by ourselves. Do it in the presence of Jesus; and, as with one hand we turn over and over the foldings and wrappings of our desperately wicked heart, let the other hand hold firmly by the skirts of His robe. Nay, study our sins, not as lying on our head merely, but as laid by God upon the head of our Saviour, as all assumed by Him, and confessed by Him, and borne and atoned for by Him; and, therefore, as all blotted out to us. Only in this way can the hard, deceitful heart be made broken and contrite (Ps. li. 17); only thus can the heart be filled with the fervours of a love which, in the forgiven soul, ought to glow with a white-heat like a furnace. I think there are two statements which every healthy soul will make with the greatest readiness. *First*, Looking round him on his fellow-believers, he will say with Paul: Most assuredly I am less than the least of all saints ; in all His family God has no child so poor, so inconsistent, so troublesome, so unworthy of Him as I am. Nay, looking round on the world of sinners, he will go on to say with the same Paul: Among all sinful men, I am the ONE vilest and most sinful. *Second*, He will add : "I have been looking over my by-past life in the light of God, and when I note its sinfulness, and His unwearied kindness to me, I feel assured that there is no creature on earth on whom the God of LOVE and MERCY has lavished more of the riches of His love and mercy than on most unworthy ME." And this thought fills him with a joy that is UNSPEAKABLE, and it incites him to love God more than others, since he owes Him so much more than others. Forgiven so much, he would fain love all the more (Luke vii. 47).

4. RELIGIOUS DELUSIONS.

I BELIEVE that the way to heaven is just as straight and narrow now as ever it was; let us beware of the false gospels and easy methods of salvation which abound everywhere. In Jeremiah's day, a time of great religious activity, all the prophets but himself healed the hurt of the people slightly, and preached, Peace, peace, when there was no peace at all (Jer. vi. 13, 14). And I feel persuaded that this is the curse of our own day. Men cannot be persuaded that the gate to life is strait, the way narrow (Matt. vii. 13, 14; 1 Pet. iv. 18). Only think of it; in Jeremiah's day, just after the great revival of religion under King Josiah, with the holy city Jerusalem full of religious men, the Lord tells the prophet that if he could find in the great city ONE SINGLE MAN who was not self-deceived, he would, for that man's sake, spare the whole nation (see Jer. v. 1, &c.). Oh, how such startling words make one tighten his grip on the hand of the Blessed Saviour, in whom ALONE is there ANY hope for us.

We are too apt to forget that the devil can be very religious, and that, in a land like ours, he works as ruinously in the form of an angel of light

as he does by tempting to coarse wickedness
(2 Cor. xi. 13, 14) ; and so attractive and plau-
sible are his religious delusions that they would
deceive even the very elect, IF THAT WERE
POSSIBLE (Matt. xxiv. 24). But God preserves
His own.

The salvation which the Lord Jesus and His
apostles preached was anything rather than *easy*.
It was easy enough to GET, for God giveth so
readily ; but it is hard, HARD to TAKE, for he who
taketh it must deny self, which is very hard ; take
up his CROSS and follow Jesus (Luke ix. 23) in His
life of utter devotedness to the holy will of God.
God's gate to heaven is very strait, and His way is
very narrow. No feet but the feet of faith can
tread therein ; TRUE faith, that faith which is His
own gift (Eph. ii. 8), that faith which is the
operation of God in the regenerated soul (Col. ii.
12); true faith, which is afraid of nothing so
much as sin, and hungers for nothing as much as
God's presence, and, abhorring nothing so much as
the fallen self-life, goes forward leaning in utter
weakness on the Beloved, trusting Him utterly,
forsaking ALL at His bidding (Luke xiv. 33), but
finding more than ALL in Him. In this way
faith journeys on in *peace* and perfect *safety*.

Let Christ be *everything* to us — EVERYTHING.
Not *something* — not much; not *very much;*
but ALL (Col. iii. 11); our " Alpha and Omega,"
our first and our last, our beginning, and middle,
and end.

CHAPTER X.

PRAYER.

1. Its Importance.

PRAYER is a subject of the greatest importance, and one that is always seasonable; and I do not know one in regard to which prevalent notions are more imperfect. Oh, what marvellous revelations the Word of God makes to us of the privilege, the delight, the power, and the value of TRUE PRAYER! It is the first and chief instrument of the Christian worker (Acts vi. 4). May the Lord grant us, IN THE FULLEST MEASURE, the spirit of true prayer; and cheerfully to leave in His hands *everything* as He pleases to arrange it.

We begin work at the right end when we begin with prayer. We are never fully realising our dependence on God, and our true calling as HIS INSTRUMENTS, unless our working and our praying be so vitally blended that we shall go to our work from our knees, and shall return from our work to our knees again. And what encouragement we have to persevering prayer for the preaching of the Gospel; we may, in our place and measure, appropriate the ministry and the promise given to our crowned Head in heaven, when His Father says to Him as in Ps. ii. 8, "ASK OF ME, and I WILL GIVE THEE the heathen for Thine inheritance." And as our faith realises Him — the Anointed Intercessor — NOW exercising this very ministry and pleading this very promise in heaven, we, His members down here on earth, anointed too with His Spirit, add our supplications, and pray with Him. For the Father is willing to give; but NOT TO GIVE UNASKED.

Hence we read in the close of Matt. ix., that our Lord, when He looked abroad over the desolate people, melted and yearned with compassion towards them, and set His disciples—what to do? Why, in the meantime, ONLY TO PRAY.

And He sets you, and me, and all of us to the same blessed work. After this manner pray ye, saying, "Our Father who art in Heaven, THY KINGDOM COME." Praying for this is laid upon the saint at all times, as his very first and foremost duty. "I exhort, therefore, that, FIRST OF ALL, supplications, prayers, intercessions, and giving of thanks, be made for all men" (1 Tim. ii. 1). And this "first of all"—that is, in the chief and foremost place, the word rendered first being the same word that in chap. i. 15 is rendered " CHIEF."

Our Anglo-Saxon race with its immense energy is prone to overlook this, and to overdo vigorous working; but God means both prayer and labour, but especially the vigorous loving faith that combines the two and "LABOURS IN PRAYER" (Col. iv. 12). The original word here rendered "labouring" is very emphatic; it is really "agonising" for you in prayer, such a vehement exercise of the whole soul that it is like the struggle of a wrestler in the arena. The same word " AGONISE " is rendered "strive" in Luke xiii. 24. Oh, may God deliver us altogether from the sin and curse of listless praying! Faith wrestles, and must do so, for where the Holy Spirit helps to pray, He excites to "*groanings* that CANNOT be uttered" (Rom. viii. 26). Its cry is, "Hear me, *lest I die*" (Ps. xiii. 3); for the believing man is *heart-broken* with his longings (Ps. cxix. 20). But formal unbelief merely babbles and maunders. And how sadly, too, does this listless praying speak of lack of love! Oh, how love pleads, and intercedes, and weeps, and wrestles! See the afflicted Syrophenician for her child, "Have mercy ON ME, O Lord; my daughter is so and so" (Matt. xv. 22). May God help us and all His children to look at things around us and to see them as the blessed Saviour does, and to yearn and feel about them with the "bowels of Jesus Christ" (Phil. i. 8), and this shall keep the spirit of prayer at the proper pitch.

I do believe there is very little spiritual bless-ing ever obtained without prayer (there is abundance of temporal mercy without it); but I believe, equally, that there is no true prayer without bless-ing. God delights to give true good; but for our sakes He must withhold it, unless we be in the proper attitude to receive it with safety to ourselves. And this attitude is on our knees, feeling our dependence, and exercising joyous and resigned trust. "You fear there is much that passes for prayer in these days, which is not prayer at all." Oh, my brother, I dare not say what I feel on this matter; the thoughts of it fill me with grief, shame, and pity. And when I feel in my own heart the strong and almost irresistible (irresistible to every power save that of the Holy Spirit's omnipotent grace, and even then, only when accompanied by my own vigilant watchfulness) tendency to sink down into the hideous depths, in which one mocks God with "prayerless praying," I get indeed a glimpse of the awful depravity of our fallen nature. And when I see so many around me who seem never to have made any discovery in this direction, I cannot but be grieved for the darkness of soul which precludes a further advance in the Divine life.

The fact is, all genuine prayer is the work of the Spirit of God (Eph. vi. 18 ; Jude 20). It follows from this that the man who is destitute of the Spirit cannot pray ; it follows equally that the Christian who is walking carelessly and grieving the Spirit of God (Eph. iv. 30), and who, therefore, is fallen out of communion—this man, while in this state of soul, may utter any amount of beautiful words ; but this is not praying.

How encouraging to the diffident, humble, believing soul, conscious of its unworthiness and of its impotence, to know that he has *one Intercessor* in Heaven to present and to endorse his prayers (Rom. viii. 34) ; while equally he has *another Intercessor* within his heart to excite and to maintain the vigorous exercise of genuine prayer ! This He does by teaching us what to pray for, and by exciting our desires for the boons we crave, till they reach

2:8

the fervour of unutterable groanings (Rom. viii. 26). How very different this true praying in the spirit is from formal prayer. In formal prayer the words used go far, far beyond the affections or the desires of the heart. There are big, big words in the mouth; but the heart is almost empty, or altogether empty, of corresponding affections. In the true prayer, on the other hand, it is entirely different. The desires go beyond the words; and though the words may be big words—very big indeed (even Bible words)—the heart's fervent longings go far beyond them; and so the burdened soul, not able to find words big enough to express the immensity and the intensity of its longings (see Ps. cxix. 20 as a sample), drops the words altogether, and turns to God with inarticulate groanings which cannot express their own meaning. Oh, most blessed praying! May you and I, my brother, know more of it. No music of heavenly harp is sweeter in the ear of God, than these unmusical groanings of a holy soul.

2. God's revealed Character and Purpose.

May I jot down a very few of the thoughts which I found helpful to myself on 1 Peter v. 10. You will see it is a prayer of the Apostle for the saints, and, like all right prayer, it is based on two things : First, the revealed character of God, as the " God of all grace ; " and second, on the revealed purpose of God, as having " called us," etc. Oh, let us see that we base all our prayers on these same *two* points : God's revealed *character* and *purpose ;* and we shall get what we ask, and the getting of it shall be safe for us.

And what a sweet name he gives to God ! He is the God of ALL grace. Everything that is in God is a delight to faith to contemplate. His omnipotence is dreadful to His enemies, but it is a delightful thought to faith, for His omnipotence is the servant of His grace. It twines its Almighty arms around us, and it says, " Fear nothing ; he that toucheth you toucheth the apple of Mine eye." And so with every attribute of God—they are all terrible to His enemies, but all delightful to His children. They are the attributes of One who is to us " the God of ALL GRACE." He who spared not, for our sakes, His beloved Son, has love enough to grudge us nothing else.

And then the Apostle goes on to found his prayer on the revealed purpose of God; and his prayer is for things which are indispensably needed for the carrying out of that gracious purpose. And this purpose is to bring us to His own eternal glory by Christ Jesus (1 Cor. i. 9). To this He has called us outwardly by His Gospel, and inwardly by the effectual calling of the Holy Spirit. And think of what this calling invites us to; think of it till our hearts grow hot within us, and as we muse the heart burns. Oh, it were infinite grace to forgive us merely; but that, besides this, we should be ACCEPTED; nay, more, accepted IN THE BELOVED (Eph. i. 6); that we should be called to glory, to share the very glory of the Lord Jesus (John xvii. 22), which glory is the glory of the Father (John xvii. 5) — all this overpowers the musing heart. Eye hath not seen it, nor ear heard it, nor heart conceived it (1 Cor. ii. 9, 10); and when we try to declare it, we can only speak like little children who know not the meaning of the immense words they speak.

Let us note one aspect of this glory: It is ETERNAL. In this it contrasts with our present sufferings, which are but for a while. If we be tried, then, because of the sharp thorns which lie plentifully on our path, and often pierce our feet, let us encourage ourselves with the thought that the eternal glory into which our Father is leading us in His love, lies beyond these thorns, and that we cannot reach it without passing through them. And leaning on the Beloved, whose path was so much thornier than ours, let us set down our naked feet on their sharp prickles with the courage of persons who are reckoning that the sufferings of this present time are not worthy to be compared with the glory which shall be revealed in us (Rom. viii. 18).

And let us note the description here given us of a Christian's present life. It is a suffering for a while. How vain to expect anything else, and how foolish to desire it. I believe it to be impossible that any soul could be brought to partake of the glory of Christ without having to drink, more or less deeply, of His cup of sorrow ; and the one shall be in proportion to the other. Hence the solemn words of 2 Tim. ii. 11–13, which are so little laid to heart.

Let us notice, too, that in praying for these beloved ones, Peter never thinks of asking that their fiery trial might be withdrawn from them, or even that it might be abated in its severity. He asks that they be STRENGTHENED to endure it; and that they be perfected and stablished through its blessed exercise. And let us take heed not to pray for exemption from the Cross; let us ask only for faith and patience. And what an abatement of the pang is it to be persuaded that the suffering is but for a little, while its glorious results shall be for ever (see 2 Cor. iv. 17, 18). At the very best we are here but strangers in a distant land—this world is only an Egypt to us, our home is in Canaan.

I will only remark that it does not seem to have occurred to Peter that there were any of those to whom he was writing who were already perfect, and did not need to be so prayed for. Nor did Paul, when he prayed for the Hebrew saints (as in Heb. xiii. 20, 21), seem to dream that any among them had already reached perfection. As for Paul himself, he had not (Phil. iii. 12). He modestly says, "Pray for us, for we trust we have a good conscience, in all things willing to live honestly."

CHAPTER XI.

THE TWO ADAMS.

THE Apostle (in Rom. v. 12–21; 1 Cor. xv. 45, 50) speaks of two men—ADAM and CHRIST—whom he sets before us as related to ourselves in a very peculiar way. In fact, he calls Christ the LAST Adam, and also the SECOND Man or Adam, which shows that there is some connection between the two men. This connection is spoken of thus: The FIRST Adam was the FIGURE of the Second—the FIGURE of Him that was to come. Let us try, then, to get some light for our practical walk from what is here told us about these TWO MEN; and may the Holy Spirit open our eyes to see and our hearts to feed upon the wonders of His Word.

God's method of dealing with man has all along been to deal with him through a Federal or Covenant HEAD. Man, if blessed at all, was to be blessed

IN HIS COVENANT HEAD. The original head was
Adam, and we were all to have been accepted as
righteous in Adam's righteousness IF HE HAD
STOOD; or now, since Adam has fallen, we may be
accepted as righteous IN CHRIST'S RIGHTEOUSNESS;
but under no dispensation could any one have
been accepted by himself. And the grand point
which we have got to settle is this : Seeing that
Adam, our head, in ruining himself has equally
ruined US, and seeing that God in His wonderful
grace has given us His own Son to be our
SECOND HEAD, who should accomplish a perfect
RIGHTEOUSNESS, the question pressed on us
for our individual settlement is, WHICH OF THE TWO
HEADS DO WE CHOOSE TO ACCEPT AS OUR ONLY
HEAD? Shall we give up totally the old life of the
Adam nature, with all its tendencies, pursuits,
and enjoyments; all its sins, its sorrows, and its
pleasures; all its self-will, its self-seeking, its self-
indulgence, and shall we, instead, consent to enter
into the Christ-life, with its humility, its trust in
God, its devoted obedience to the Father, its
joyous submission to His WILL, and its delighted
rest in His love—shall SELF be EVERYTHING
to us as it was to Adam in his fall, or shall GOD
be EVERYTHING to us, AS HE WAS TO JESUS ?

The subject is too immense to do any more than merely glance at it, but I am overwhelmed with wonder at the infinite love shown in all this amazing scheme for fallen, ruined man's recovery.

Before ever our first Father had been created, God, foreseeing that, though the test of obedience to which he would be subjected was a very easy one, he would nevertheless fall, had ALREADY ARRANGED to provide for us a SECOND HEAD, even His own CO-EQUAL SON, who, as MAN, should atone for the guilt of the first Adam, should abundantly repair all the damage; nay, should make it many-fold better for the SAVED IN CHRIST than it would have been, even if they had not been lost in Adam. And now the Gospel puts before each of us the simple choice, whether, having been ruined by our FIRST HEAD, and having tasted something of the bitterness of that ruin, we shall CONSENT to GIVE UP ENTIRELY this wretched sin-cursed nature, and receive instead the holy and eternally - blessed nature provided for us, at infinite cost, by the living and dying obedience of the SECOND ADAM, the incarnate Son of God. IN CHRIST or IN ADAM, that settles our everlasting condition ; and every man is in Christ who willingly accepts Him, while every one is in Adam who neglects, or refuses to make this choice. And when we find the mournful workings of an evil heart in ourselves this should humble us, but not discourage us, for the evil heart belongs to the old Adam life, which we still bear about with us while we are here, and not to the Christ-life, which becomes our life when we accept it.

CHAPTER XII.

THE TWO NATURES.

THERE are in the believer two natures, the one entirely opposed to the other. Tho one nature CANNOT obey God (Rom. viii. 7, 8), the other CANNOT disobey Him (1 John iii. 9). The old nature cannot believe, cannot love God, cannot deny itself—all these are utterly impossible to it ; while the new nature CANNOT BUT live in faith, and love, and self-denial. Now, all this involves an irreconcilable opposition within the heart of the saint. The old nature strives against everything that the new nature proposes to do, while the new nature strives against everything that the old wants to get done; for the two natures are contrary, the one to the other, and so the man cannot get, or at least he finds it difficult to get, anything done easily. So the apostle teaches us in Gal. v. 17.

Now, how much sorrow, almost even near to

despair, would the clear understanding of all this spare many an humble but imperfectly instructed child of God. He had thought that when converted he would henceforward be all light, all love, all holiness, all happiness, with nothing in him that should oppose God any more; but he finds, in experience, that matters are as different from this as possible. He has an opportunity for private prayer, but he feels a strange reluctance to avail himself of it; or, if he do avail himself, how distracted his mind becomes with wandering thoughts. He would spend a little while in reading the Bible, and in meditating on what he reads, but he cannot get into it as he easily gets into the spirit of the newspaper. Perhaps his very sweetest enjoyments that he can remember have been favoured seasons of communion with God, when, whether out of the body or in the body, he scarce could tell; and yet, when he would fain renew these sweet experiences, how strangely is he hindered—his soul seems to struggle like a caged bird against the wires of its cage, through which it cannot pass.

Because of these, and other similar experiences, the man ofttimes gets sorely distressed. He writes mercilessly bitter things against himself, and winds

up with saying : "It is impossible that I can be a
new man, a child of God, for my heart is like a
cage of unclean birds." Indeed it is so, and the
man ought to be deeply humbled because it is so.
He should, like Job, "ABHOR HIMSELF" for it, or
like penitents in all ages "LOATHE HIMSELF"; but
there is no reason that he should think himself a
reprobate. His heart is as bad as he thinks it to
be, and far, FAR worse, but it was always so. Conversion has not changed it in the least ; it has given
him a new nature, and LEFT THE OLD AS IT WAS.
He has two natures now, and it is this new man in
him which is to rule, ay, and to crucify the sin-
loving old man (Gal. v. 24). But to expect that
the old nature will cease to hate TRUE prayer, or
be brought to find delight in genuine communion
with God, is to mistake the whole matter. Just as
reasonably might one try to persuade Satan to join
him in prayer, or in true spiritual fellowship with
God. No, we need to USE FORCE AGAINST OUR
OWN FLESH, to knock down our opposing self, as it
were, and striding over it, lay eager hold on Jesus.
And this we are quite able to do. If we have faith
enough to rise up to the resolution, Christ will give
us strength (Matt. xvii. 20 ; 2 Cor. xii. 9, 10).

Since there are two natures in the saint, it is of

great importance, practically, which of the two he yields to. With the sinner there is no difficulty, for he has but one nature. But in a regenerated man there are two; and, unless he understand this, many precious words of Scripture will be a puzzle to him; and they shall probably be perverted. As for the old man in the saint, God does not look on it, nor treat it as His child, but as HIS irreconcilable enemy. He has sentenced it to destruction; meanwhile, His treatment of His child, as for the time a very strangely compounded personality, is designed to nurture and strengthen the seed of God in him, and to dishearten and weaken the old man. Let us seek to fall in with God's thoughts, and act in precisely the same way. We have died to the old self, and must now deny, resist, and mortify it with all our might. Paul did so (1 Cor. ix. 27). Whatever serves the interests of the new man, we should prize most highly; and this none the less that it grieves, and robs, and sorely hurts the old man.

It is a wonderful subject, humbling, comforting, stimulating; and I cannot tell you how much I like to lie and muse on these stupendous themes. I am afraid that I have not made it sufficiently plain, but must conclude for the present.

CHAPTER XIII.

GREAT NEED AND GREAT SUPPLY.

IN thinking of our sinfulness, we are too ready to forget the great sin — the sin of our NATURE. It is this which constitutes the most frightful part of our guilt. WHAT we ARE is of far more consequence to us than anything we have DONE. It was this thought that broke the heart of penitent David, when, bewailing his horrible crimes of murder and seduction, he connected the acts with the nature out of which they sprung, and said, "Behold I was shapen in iniquity, and in sin did my mother conceive me" (Ps. li. 5). For, by nature, we are dead, DEAD in trespasses and sins ; and this is a much worse case than the being guilty of occasional offences against the holy law of God.

How wonderfully fitted Christ and ourselves are for one another. *We* need such a Saviour, one who is able to SAVE TO THE UTTERMOST all who come

unto God by Him (Heb. vii. 25). And HE NEEDS
JUST SUCH SINNERS as we are; for, how otherwise
could He show forth the EXCEEDING RICHES OF THE
FATHER'S GRACE (Eph. ii. 7) if there were no
needy, and perishing, and utterly undone sinners,
on whom to show it forth? And let this thought
encourage us the more to trust Him UTTERLY.
His end being MERCY, we suit His purpose as
perfectly as He suits our necessity. As the saying
is, such a Saviour and such sinners are well met.

God has His glory; and it lies in His infinite
fulness of every good. There is none good but
ONE; that is GOD. All the good in the universe is
His alone. But we too have our glory—a very
different one from God's. It lies in the immense
capacity of our souls (and they are inconceivably
capacious), while these capacious souls are utterly
empty. We have nothing of our own wherewith to
fill them; and all the worlds in creation would not
satisfy the intensity of their hunger. And God
gave us this immense capacity of soul, just that we
might need Him, might hunger and thirst with
famine-pangs for the living God. And when we
are brought to do so, then He has the glory of filling up our emptiness out of His own fulness;
while we have the unequalled joy of being filled

with all the fulness of God (Eph. iii. 19). And
so the larger any soul is, and the more COMPLETELY
EMPTY IT IS, the more blessed is the man; for
his intense hunger constrains him the more readily
to resort to Christ, while, also, there is more room
in him to receive of the Divine fulness.   And then
the man's cup runneth over (Ps. xxiii. 5).

But, alas ! God finds comparatively few souls
that are empty.   Most are filled with self, and
with the trash of this world ; and though they may
be hungry, even to famishing, it is not after God,
but after more of the lust of the eye, the lust of
the flesh, and the pride of life.   And when religiously
inclined, their heart is occupied with religious
doctrines, church systems, ordinances, and contro-
versies ; and also an immense amount of self-
righteousness.

Oh, how blessed are they whom God has completely emptied of all these things ! whose word is,
" As the hart panteth after the water-brooks, so
panteth my soul after THEE, O GOD.   My soul
thirsteth FOR GOD, for the Living GOD ; when
shall I come and appear before God ? " (Ps. xlii.
1, 2).   Blessed are they who thus hunger and thirst,
for they SHALL BE FILLED (Matt. v. 6).

Let us fall in with His loving purposes about us,
2:9

and let us give Him what to Him is an unequalled joy, the joy of finding in each of us a great capacious heart, able to hold much, but completely emptied, and hungering and thirsting, sighing and crying to be FILLED WITH HIMSELF.   And when we do so, He shall open windows in heaven over our heads, and shall pour down on us such blessings as the largest heart shall not be able to take in (Mal. iii. 10).   This is FAITH, this *receptiveness* of heart for GOD.

CHAPTER XIV.

TWO PAIRS OF EYES.

THE Christian has two pairs of eyes, and we are apt to look at things sometimes through one pair, and sometimes through the other pair, and sometimes through them both at once. We have the eyes of Nature, which do well enough for this world's things, but which, when used to look at God, and the things of God, see all these things in the falsest light possible. They put darkness for light, and light for darkness; they count good to be evil, and evil to be good. And it is just because the natural man walks by the guidance of his natural eyes, that he continues to be the godless, worldly, sinful creature that he is.

But God has given us another pair of eyes, the eyes of faith. By means of them we see into another world of things altogether. And what we see by the eyes of faith are all true, for they are

seen in the clear light of GOD Himself.   Now, as
Christians, we are meant to CLOSE the first pair of
eyes, and to put them to no use whatever except
in what concerns this world's work; and we are
meant, in regard to everything else, to open the
second pair of eyes, the eyes of FAITH, and to walk
by what they see.   And it is simply because most of
us persist in looking at things with BOTH pairs of
eyes (instead of with one pair ALONE), that our
walk is so inconsistent and unsteady, and our
spirits so feeble and troubled.   Oh, let us pray for,
and aim after, the SINGLE EYE, which keeps the
whole man FULL of heaven's own light; for without this singleness of eye our very light shall be
darkness (Matt. vi. 23; compare 2 Cor. iv. 16–
18; v. 7; Heb. xi. 27).

And the great object with which this eye of
Faith is occupied, is GOD HIMSELF.   The man sets
the LORD ever before him, and because he feels his
Divine keeper to be on his right hand, nothing can
greatly move him.   And though, of course, he has
to look on the persons and things around him,
yet, as he does so only through his new pair of
eyes, and in the light of God, they all look so
differently to him.   For instance, when a man
looks at some great loss, or some affliction, through

his natural eyes, then he sees it to be a great evil, and he frets and murmurs, and becomes more sinful and miserable because of it. But when another man looks at a similar trouble through the eyes of faith, oh, how differently he sees things! He sees the great GOD thinking over the case of himself, a poor and needy one (Ps. xl. 17); he sees his trusted and most loving Father picking out of His treasury, as it were, the most precious thing He can find in it, that He may send it as a love-gift to a dearly beloved child; and he sees God choosing this very affliction for him, and sending it to him in pure love, and for his highest good. And knowing that his Father cannot be MISTAKEN so as to make a wrong choice, he welcomes the precious gift; and he is careful, above all, not to look at it with his old natural eyes, for he knows that if he did so, the sight would lead him into sin against GOD, and into much misery in his own soul. But when he looks at God, and on the things of God, and on himself in his true relation to God, with the eyes of faith, oh, how blessed and how enjoyable everything becomes! With Him beside us, pain and sickness are as acceptable as ease and health. For His smile is EVERYTHING to us, and possessing that, we

can afford to let all else go (Hab. iii. 17–19).
Indeed, as a matter of fact, the children of God
enjoy His presence far more in the absence of
outward comforts, than in the possession of them;
and so, when our Father sees that we are so feeble
that we need the outward mercy to help us to
enjoy Himself, He gives us the outward mercy;
but, when He sees that we could enjoy Him far
more without the intervention of the creature
mercy, then He takes it away, for we are so apt
to lean on it. And those who trust Him make
up for the loss of the creature by drawing their
consolation more directly from HIMSELF.

CHAPTER XV.

THE HOLY SPIRIT.

1. His Work in Believers.

OUR blessed Lord spoke to the apostles, after His resurrection, of the Holy Spirit as the promise of the Father (Acts i. 4). How much was suggested to them by this expression! For He was now to them the grand object of desire and expectation, just as the promised Christ was to ancient Israel. As a gift, the gift of the Holy Ghost includes all besides; and he who receives it receives every blessing. The other dispensations which preceded ours are all eclipsed by the present Gospel dispensation; and the matchless glory of our dispensation lies in this—the unspeakable gift of the Holy Spirit. Speaking of His own day, and comparing its privileges with those of the days that had gone before, our Lord says of it (Luke x. 23, 24): "Blessed are the eyes which

see the things that ye see; for I tell you that
many prophets and kings have desired to see those
things which ye see, and have not seen them;
and to hear those things which ye hear, and have
not heard them." But when He compares this
same day which was so far in advance of those
which had preceded it, with the days which were
to follow, He pronounces the latter to be still more
blessed; and more blessed, too, *because of the Holy
Spirit's presence.* "It is EXPEDIENT for you that
I go away; for if I go not away, the *Comforter* will
not come unto you" (John xvi. 7). The Holy
Spirit's presence within us is so much better than
even our Lord's personal presence beside us could
be. Oh, my brother, what manner of persons
ought we to be, who live in this favoured day of
the fulness of Divine grace !

A Gospel without the Holy Spirit is as imperfect
as a Gospel without Christ. Pentecost, or the
advent of the promised Spirit, is as indispensable
to the blessing of the individual, or of the Church,
as the Passover, or the dying of the Redeemer.
Without Christ there is no redemption at all, but
without the Holy Spirit we can enjoy not one of
the fruits of redemption. For whatever Christ is
to us, He is by the Holy Spirit.

How indispensable then is His Almighty help to
our living a true Christ-like life of consecration;
a life like that described by the apostle in Gal.
ii. 20. We may indeed live a formal average life
which easily passes for Christian without His
special aid, but without Him we shall never be
able to live as Christians are called to do. For on
what a pitch of holy devotedness does God mean
His recovered lost ones, His restored prodigals, to
walk henceforward before Him! Ere we can enter
on it, it is indispensable that we forsake ALL, that
we hate even our lives (Luke xiv. 26, 33). Is not
that a strait gate, my brother? Then we are to
keep the flesh *crucified*, CRUCIFIED from beginning
to end of our course (Gal. v. 24); and we are able
to do this since the Lord who bids us do it will
enable us to do it (Rom. xiv. 4). We are to pray,
not so many times a day, but "*without* CEASING"
(1 Thess. v. 17); we are to do *every* thing that
we do at all, *to the glory of God,* even down
to the animal function of eating and drinking
(1 Cor. x. 31). In one word, our whole walk
as Christians is to be on such a lofty level
that it shall be "WORTHY of the Lord Christ"
(Col. i. 10); "WORTHY of God our Father"
(1 Thess. ii. 12); "WORTHY of our calling," and

its unspeakable expectations and privileges ! (Eph. iv. 1).

Now, who is sufficient for these things? In truth, in this direction, apart from Christ working in us by His Spirit, we can do NOTHING. We are as incapable of living on a scale like this, as an animal. But then God has graciously provided for our need, and He is as able as He is willing to work *in* us far beyond our thinking (Eph. iii. 20). To work *what* in us ? Our sanctification (1 Thess. iv. 3); *only*, as He works in us, we must yield up ourselves to His blessed impulses, and, with all our diligence, *we must work out* (Phil. ii. 12, 13).

And on what an immense scale is this indispensable help accessible to us. The Holy Spirit's gracious aid is given to all who ask—to ALL, without exception. This is indubitably certain (LUKE xi. 13).

And in what fulness of grace does the Holy Spirit come to work in us. Will you, my dear brother, weigh, as I often do, the astonishing words in John vii. 37, 38, 39. Here the believer is assured not only that his thirst of soul shall be quenched, but that, infinitely more, OUT OF HIM shall flow RIVERS of living water. For God gives without stint. Speaking of the same Spirit He

promised in Isaiah xliv. 3, that in dealing with a
thirsty soul He would—what? Give him a draught
of water merely? Oh no; but, "I will POUR
WATER on him that is thirsty, and FLOODS upon
the dry ground." And by this water He signifies
His Spirit ; see the words which follow.   No
wonder, then, that we are commanded to be *filled*,
FILLED, FILLED with the Spirit (Eph. v. 18), the
very command indicating that our deficiency in
any case is due, not to His reluctant giving, but to
our reluctant accepting. How is it, then, that
though the case be so, most of us enjoy so imperfectly this rich gift of God's exceeding grace ?
Alas ! I fear that the reason is a very sad one.
When the Holy Spirit comes, He comes to convict
us of the enormous guilt of all living after the
flesh, to make us loathe ourselves because of this
life of self, to make us willing to have it destroyed,
nay, to make us divinely strong enough to destroy
it with our own hands. And we—most of us—
are so madly, wickedly set on retaining of this
"SELF LIFE," that rather than give it up we forego
the blessedness of full communion with Christ,
in the fellowship with Him of the eternal life
(1 John i. 1–3). We cannot, *we* DO NOT—most
of us—meet the indispensable preliminary require-

ment of Luke xiv. 26, 27, 33. But God will not be mocked in regard to this matter of the condemned flesh (Gal. vi. 7, 8). If we will protect and retain the flesh, then we must be without the Spirit's power; for the inexorable word of Rom. viii. 13 must be fulfilled. The flesh is already sentenced to death (Gal. v. 24).

What a wonderful thought that the Spirit of God so identifies Himself with us as He does! In carrying out *His* work, the Son of God took flesh. He came not only close to us, He did infinitely more. Because we were partakers of flesh and blood, He also took on Him flesh and blood (Heb. ii. 14). Nay, so perfectly did He identify Himself with us, that — oh! wonder beyond wonders—such a word is spoken of Him as, " made a curse for us " (Gal. iii. 13); " made to be sin for us " (2 Cor. v. 21). But just as wonderful, just as intimate is the Holy Spirit's way of identifying Himself with us. Indeed, he comes nearer to us still. For while the Divine Son united Himself to the race, the Holy Spirit enters into the individual, and takes up His final dwelling in the regenerated heart. And if the Lord Jesus be united to the individual, as He is, it is only by means of the indwelling Spirit who dwells in the

Head and in the members. And so completely does the blessed Spirit co-operate with us, that He enters into the actual feeling of our sorrows and our wants. He pours His energies into the channel of our sanctified affections, exciting in us desires and groanings, sighings and aspirations which go beyond the power of man to express. And these exercises of soul are His exercises within us as well as ours, His prayers as well as ours; and while they go up before God as *our* prayers, they go up also as *His* prayers, *His* "intercessions," His "mind" (see Rom. viii. **26, 27**).

Oh, that we may be led into a daily increasing closeness of walk with our glorified Lord, by our believing and faithful walk IN THE SPIRIT.

No wonder it is that the awe-struck, inspired apostle speaks of this salvation as "SO GREAT salvation" (Heb. ii. **3**). It is not merely a deliverance from hell, but it is a bestowal of sonship and heirship, and of union with Christ. And they shall be better secured against the danger of "NEGLECTING" it (Heb. ii. 3) who are filled with suitable apprehensions of its grandeur and glory.

2. THE SPIRIT OF POWER.

As Christians, we, like Timothy, have received from God a Spirit; so we are told what this Spirit IS NOT, and what it IS (2 Tim. i. 7).

It is not a Spirit of fear. The word means *cowardice*, and it is that used in Rev. xxi. 8; Judges vii. 3. God uses many very imperfect and faulty instruments, but He scarcely ever uses a coward or a sluggard. Timothy probably was constitutionally timid (we see as much from what is said of him), and needed this hint, but we all, and always, need it too.

The Spirit of God in a believer, then, is the Spirit of POWER (Acts i. 8; compare what is said of Stephen in Acts vi. 5, 8). Of course we must limit our conception of this POWER in the believer to the doing the will of God. We may not do everything that we please, but only what He tells us. For Christ has all power in Heaven and in earth, and WE are, when in our right place, the ORGANS of His almighty will (Matt. xxviii. 19, 20; note "THEREFORE" in verse 20). In our place, then, we are as it were just with His omnipotence (Ps. xviii. 32) ABLE to do whatever He is able to do and means to do by us (Rom. xiv. 4). Hence, when we walk *in faith*, that is, as He leads us, NOTHING, NOTHING is impossible to us (Matt. xvii. 20).

> " Faith, mighty faith the promise sees,
>   And looks to that alone ;
>   Laughs at impossibilities,
>   And says, ' It shall be done.' "

Oh, what thoughts crowd into one's mind in connection with this. Is it not POWER that we mainly need ? and here we have it. In ourselves we have none, not one particle (see John xv. 5) ; while here we have power sufficient for all our need (Phil. iv. 13). Train nature as you will, it is still " without strength." We see this in the apostles before Pentecost. What a change did Pentecost make on them. Before this, they were impotent, and yet they knew it not. " Are ye able to drink of My cup ? " etc., etc. (Matt. xx. 22), asked our Lord of John and James. " We are ABLE," they boldly answered, most sincere but most self-ignorant. And so, when the cup was presented and the baptism fell due, they forsook Him and fled for life. They were still under the spirit of " COWARDICE." And so it is with mere nature always. Let us remember that ALL our strength is in Christ (2 Cor. iii. 5).

CHAPTER XVI.

A HOLY LIFE.

IN seeking to be a faithful witness for the Lord
—I do not mean by speaking only (that, too,
of course), but by the quiet power that proceeds
out of a holy life, a life holy because spent with
God—and in seeking to maintain this, I find
failure continually from the want of *watchfulness,*
EXTRAORDINARY *watchfulness*—watchfulness above
and beyond what I have attained to. And this
watchfulness directed not so much to the great
points (though that, too), as to the seeming trifles.
Ah, it is through the little matters that Satan
attacks us and cripples us. These seeming trifles
that we so readily overlook, are to him but the
sharp point of the wedge, which, if he manage to
get once inserted, he will soon drive home, to the
breaking up of the sweetest frame of spirit, and the
splitting asunder of the most hearty decision. If

we permit SELF-WILL in the trifle, we shall soon have self-will in the weighty matters; if we permit unfaithfulness in a penny, we shall soon be pilferers of God's money by the pound. A moment's levity, or, worse still, an ungenerous word or thought about a weak brother, may do for us what the shearing of Samson's locks did for him, and leave us helpless in our enemies' hands.

We need also to cultivate a spirit of humility, but we cannot be humble without *self-knowledge*, and SELF-KNOWLEDGE is impossible without our being much in the Lord's presence, where alone we will see sin in its true light, and ourselves to be what we are. It is only the contrite, the HEART-BROKEN (whose broken hearts are healed), that God delights in (Isa. lvii. 15; lxii. 4). Oh, to be humble, most deeply humble, and to be loving, most tenderly loving, and to have *self-will* cast out and exterminated. God alone can work these in any heart. FAITH and FAITHFULNESS—faith without doubting, and faithfulness without compromising—and a heart made truly humble by being much in the Lord's presence—these are the grand elements of a holy and useful life. In order to this, there is nothing so important as COMMUNION WITH GOD. No service, NOTHING, NOTHING must be suffered

2:10

to interfere with that, "*Keep* THY HEART beyond all keeping" for out of it comes the entire life (Prov. iv. 23). I am struck with Paul's words to the Ephesian elders, "Take heed to the Church" —the Church so precious in the eyes of GOD, that He has redeemed it with His own BLOOD; the Church whose real Keeper and Guide is no less than the Holy Ghost—take heed to feed this Church as entrusted to your care; but even before you do this—*first* and *foremost*—"TAKE HEED UNTO YOUR-SELVES" (see Acts xx. 28). And similarly writing to Timothy, he says, "Take heed unto thy TEACH-ING"—it is the truth that regenerates (1 Peter i. 23); it is the truth that sanctifies (John xvii. 17). Error destroys, and where there is truth enough mixed with it to save from utter destruction, error still blights, and withers, and renders sickly. Therefore, take tremulous heed to thy *teaching*; but *before* this—even in the FIRST *and* FOREMOST place—"take heed unto THYSELF" (1 Tim. iv. 16); for God makes use only of holy vessels for holy uses (see Exodus and Leviticus everywhere).

CHAPTER XVII.

THE MIND OF CHRIST.

WE have in the simple words, " Let this mind be in you, which was also in Christ Jesus" (Phil. ii. 5), a condensed summary of Christian duty. We need aim at, and pray for, nothing else; it is enough that we think and feel, speak and act, AS CHRIST DID.

The lesson pressed on us includes in it *humility*, but it includes much besides. We have humility referred to in verse 3, and deep, fervent, self-sacrificing love in verses 2 and 4, and the most unreserved obedience to the will of God in verses 6, 7, and 8 ; and all these, as Christians, we are to carry out by the help of God's Spirit in the fullest measure.

It is also much more than the mere example of Christ that is pressed on us. Example is more or less of an outward thing, but the thing enjoined

147

here is inward—it is the cherishing of the same
mind or spirit that He had ; and then, of course,
our outward walk shall resemble His.   His mind
was filled with consuming zeal for the holy law of
God in both its tables—perfect love to God, and
also perfect love to man (Matt. xxii. 37–39)—and
this engrossing love led Him, at all costs to Himself,
to serve the will of God, and to seek the welfare of
men.   Everything belonging to Himself He freely
sacrificed for these.   Now do you, O Philippians,
cherish the same disposition !   Let the same zeal
of love to God and man burn like a coal in your
hearts, and you, too, shall walk in obedience to
God, and in most loving service to your fellow-
men.   This is your calling as Christians (1 John
ii. 6 ; Col. ii. 6).   To enable you to do this, the
Holy Spirit has been given you.   And so indispensable is it that you have the Spirit of Christ,
and also that you give yourself up to His leading,
that, if you have Him not, you don't belong to
Christ at all (Rom. viii. 9–14).   In fact, it is the
possession of this mind of Christ, or Spirit of
Christ, or new nature in Christ, that constitutes in
the full sense SALVATION.   And, having at first
received this salvation, we are to go on and work
out this salvation with fear and trembling, enabled

to do so by God's Divine operation within us (Phil. ii. 12, 13) ; for there is no rest in any degree of attainment here. Paul at this moment, when writing, was a chained prisoner, and was in danger of a violent death any day ; but such was his self-sacrificing love for God and man, that he thinks with pleasure of his being killed for his obedience to the one, and for the benefit of the other, and speaks of such death as in chapter ii. 17, 18. This was a high point of attainment ; but in chapter i. 21 we see he had attained one still higher. And yet, so far from being satisfied with what (through grace) he had reached, he forgot it all, counted it as nothing, and pressed eagerly onward to attain still more of the same self-sacrificing mind that was in Christ (read chapter iii. 12, 13, 14).

The same course he urges upon all disciples (chapter iii. 15, 16, 17). There were some, how-ever, who manifested none of this spirit, who, though Christians so called (aye, and teachers), lived for SELF and not for God, for SELF and not for others ; but their self-indulgent spirit showed them to be no members of Christ, and, therefore, they would never reach glory as Christ reached it (chapter ii. 9), but " whose end was destruction " (chapter iii. 18, 19). The apostle weeps as he thinks of their deplorable condition and harmful influence.

And alas, alas, even in Paul's day there were not many of Paul's spirit. Paul had one companion, at least, in whose true communion he had much joy; it was Timothy. Will you read what he says of others in chapter ii. 20, 21? There was but one Timothy, no more; but there were "MANY" of the stamp spoken of in chapter iii. 18. Ah, my brother, it is not so easy to be an out-and-out Christian, as many suppose, nor so common; the popular estimate on this matter is dreadfully wrong.

There have been on earth only two *fontal* lives— lives out of which all other human lives flow as a stream flows out of its fountain; two, and no more. These are Adam and Christ. Every human life is a *repetition*, or, if you will, a continuation of the one or of the other of these two lives. By first birth we all receive the fallen nature of Adam; by new birth, REGENERATION, as we call it, true believers receive the new nature (2 Pet. i. 4; 1 John i. 1–3; Col. iii. 1–4, etc., etc.). Dead in ourselves, we are made alive IN CHRIST (Eph. ii. 1–5). It is by the Holy Spirit that this *quickening* is effected; and it is by the same Holy Spirit's continued indwelling that the quickened man is enabled to walk as one who has the " SAME MIND " that was also in Christ. And it is the possession of this Spirit, with the consequent walking as He leads, that constitutes salvation in the fullest sense.

All who are in Adam are still dead in trespasses and sins ; they, and they alone, who are led by the Spirit of God are the sons of God (Rom. viii. 14). The very nature of the Adam-life, the self-life in us all, is to seek our own things, our pleasure, or profit, or will, and to sacrifice for sake of attaining them, not only the welfare of others but the glory of God. The very nature of the second Adam, the new creation, the regenerated spirit, is the direct opposite. It constrains a man, so far as he cherishes it, to love God, so that, like Christ, he shall sacrifice all that concerns himself to serve the will of God ; and to love man, so that to secure another's welfare shall be as dear to him as to secure his own (Phil. ii. 3, 4 ; 1 Cor. x. 24, 33). This is OUR CALLING as members of Christ. To cultivate this new life we need to suppress, to mortify, the old (Rom. viii. 13 ; Gal. v. 24; Col. iii. 4, 5). And to mortify the one life while we carefully, prayerfully cherish the other, is the ONE GRAND SERVICE of every

Christian for the present.   Will you carefully note
the force of the word " ONLY " in Phil. i. 27, and
of the word " THIS ONE THING I do " in chapter iii.
13.

From first to last, all our salvation is in Christ.
We have nothing, are nothing, can do nothing
apart from Him.   But grace reigneth, and it is
His delight to give.   Does any man try to subdue
his reigning selfishness, to put it away, and to live
in love—a love like God's own love ?   If so, he
soon finds out that it is difficult, nay, that it is
impossible.   The very motive that sets him on
seeking this, is itself a selfish one.   He cannot, by
his utmost effort, free himself from the reigning
power of selfishness in his mind and heart, any
more than he can free his body from the grasp of
the law of gravity.   But here God's wonderful
provision in the Gospel comes in to supply our
need.   The same Son of God, who assumed flesh,
and who bore the guilt of our sins upon the Cross,
that by His atoning sacrifice He might make it a
righteous thing for God to forgive us fully and
freely, does more for us than this.   He is ready to
come into the heart of the believing, struggling
man, and to live in him, in order to deliver the
man from the all-controlling dominion of his sin,

that is, of his SELFISHNESS. For this very end the Holy Spirit has come, and it is the receiving of, and the walking in, this Holy Spirit that constitutes one great difference between those who are really saved and those who are not. If, then, we have any measure of Divine light in us, so as to desire Christ and union with Him beyond all else, the assurance and the promise of grace like this shall be delightful news to us, and we shall seek the fullest enjoyment of this peerless blessing. And to encourage us to seek it, and to seek increase of it, let us remember that God bestows this boon on all who ask it more readily than tender earthly parents ever give food to their hungry child. If any one be without it, the hindrance lies with himself, not with God (Luke xi. 13).

But unless we cultivate this mind that was in Christ (Phil. ii. 5), our fleshly walking shall GRIEVE the Spirit (Eph. iv. 30), and we shall, as a result, have His grace more and more withheld.

God is LOVE, and Christ is incarnate God—that is, INCARNATE LOVE. The Holy Spirit is the spirit of love, and His first fruit in the renewed heart is LOVE (Gal. v. 22). The Gospel is the most wonderful exhibition of Divine love that is conceivable. Now, love always assimilates the subjects of it, when it so happens that they are unlike each other. For when two parties love each other, they are both unhappy if any strong dissimilarity exists between them. The love will powerfully constrain them to seek a perfect similarity of character, and this it will do in proportion to its intensity. It were no love if it did not so operate. But this assimilative energy will act in one or other of two ways, according to the relative position of the parties. If the one be much more exalted than the other, his love will set him on seeking to have the inferior, whom he loves, to be like himself; and, *so far as he can*, he will communicate to this inferior every help towards the attainment of the excellences which go to form his own superiority; will he not? On the other hand, in the case of the inferior, his love will set him on aiming at the excellences of the superior, and he will use diligently every help afforded him for this end. And this he will do, not from selfish motives but from LOVE, that he may resemble the beloved superior, and that he may not grieve him by sight of his own unlovely evils. Now, apply all this to Christ and ourselves; just AS He loves us, so does He desire to make us like Himself, and AS WE love Him, *so* FAR, too, do we desire and seek to be made like Him. So His love works in us to will and to do, while our love to Him stirs us up to work out in response to His working within (Phil. ii. 12, 13). And this is salvation, as God intends that we now enjoy it.

Christ for us on the Cross, Christ for us on the throne, Christ in us by His Spirit ; and we cannot afford to overlook any one of the three.

CHAPTER XVIII.

CHRIST FORMED IN US.

I HAVE just been hanging over a verse in one
of Paul's epistles, trying to get my soul steeped
and satisfied with its humbling, sanctifying truth.
I had been reading Gal. iv., and verse 19 took
hold of my mind. How very tenderly he speaks
to the Galatians; and this seems the more striking
when we remember their spiritual condition at this
moment. They were acting like bewitched fools
(chapter iii. 1), for they were turning aside from
Christ to another gospel (chapter i. 6, 7). Of
course the Apostle was deeply grieved, but his love
suffers no abatement, they are " MY LITTLE CHILD-
REN." It never occurred to him to abandon them
for their backsliding, love will not readily think of
that course.

We see here also what it really is to be a
Christian. It is to have CHRIST FORMED IN US—

THIS, and nothing else, and *nothing* LESS.   It
is to be in a condition of which this is the true
description, " To ME TO LIVE IS CHRIST " (Phil.
i. 21); "I live, YET NOT I, but CHRIST LIVETH
IN ME " (Gal. ii. 20).   Alas, how sadly below
anything like this does the popular conception everywhere of what constitutes a Christian
fall !

We see, too, what is God's grand end in insti-
tuting ministry, and in appointing ordinances.   It
is that Christ may be thus formed in hearts
where heretofore He has not been, and may
be more perfectly formed in those who already
enjoy His indwelling ; to give life to the dead,
and more abundant life to the living (John
x. 10).

We see also, in a most affecting way, what is
the spirit in which all ministry is to be carried
out by every one who is entrusted with it ; and
we are all entrusted with some form of ministry
or other.   This spirit is spoken of as the very
anguish of a mother in her birth-pangs.   For the
true minister has himself the Christ living in
him, and acting through him ; and, therefore, he
yearns over souls with the very bowels of Jesus
Christ (Phil. i. 8).

And we see, too, that these gracious sorrows, these pangs of holy anguish, are continued till the desired end is reached—until Christ be formed in the souls of the beloved and longed-for.   Short of this there is no rest, and all ministry falls very short that is not carried out in this spirit.   See another strong word of Paul in Rom. ix. 1–3 ; see Jeremiah's weeping (Jer. ix. 1) ; see David's floods of tears and horror of soul (Ps. cxix. 136, 53) ; see the Church's anguish as contrasted with the world's joy during the entire dispensation (John xvi. 20–22).

Since then the Lord has instituted all ministry, and appointed all ordinances with this end, that Christ should be formed in us, with what " VEHE-MENT DESIRE " should we set ourselves to have this gracious purpose PERFECTLY accomplished in ourselves—to live purely and simply by the grace of the indwelling Son of God ?   So did this same Paul, who had already attained so much, forget all the past, and press with insatiable ardour after a fuller attainment (Phil. iii. 8–14).   In this eager pursuit he treated his obstructing body as a very enemy (1 Cor. ix. 27).   I am struck with the strong expressions of holy desire in respect to this, uttered even under the old economy (see Ps. xlii.

1; lxiii. 1; lxxxiv. 1, 2). Think of a man's
heart " BREAKING," actually " BREAKING," with these
precious desires (Ps. cxix. 20; compare Matt. v. 6).
And while we thus earnestly covet God's best gift
for ourselves, should we not also travail in Paul-
like birth-pangs for the blessing of beloved ones
dear to us by natural ties? God has surely laid
them very specially on our hearts. Like Jacob at
Jabbok for his wives and children, should we not
find a very Jabbok ofttimes, and in many places?
In short, should we not thus travail in very
agonies of spirit for ALL SAINTS and for all SINNERS,
especially for those who are personally known to
us? Our God lays it on us to plead thus with
our uttermost intensity for " ALL SAINTS " (Eph.
vi. 18). And He commits to us as our *very* FIRST
service, " FIRST OF ALL," that we should thus inter-
cede for " ALL MEN " (1 Tim. ii. 1). And the
spirit in which these intercessions are meant to
be carried on is indicated to us by such a passage
as Col. iv. 12, where the word rendered " labouring fervently" is really the Greek word "agonising."
" Epaphras, who is one of you, a servant of Christ,
saluteth you, always agonising for you in prayers
that ye may stand perfect and complete in all the
will of God."

And if we really love our neighbour as ourselves, shall not his soul be dear to us as our own ;
and shall we not groan and wrestle and agonise in
exercises of spirit resembling a mother's birth-
pangs, for his full blessing, as we would for our
own ?   And if we love our brother, as we delight
to think THE LORD LOVES OURSELVES (and this
is the standard which is set before us, John xiii.
34), how shall it be possible for us to avoid these
holy agonies on his behalf ?   We are expected to
be able and willing to lay down our lives for him,
in a love like Christ's own love (1 John iii. 16).
And it is very certain that love on a pitch like
this shall secure sorrows and travail-pangs like
those of the holy apostle.   Does not our apathy,
our coldness in this respect, indicate how little
faith we really have, how little love, how little
true grace of any kind; in one word, how
feebly most of us enjoy the energetic presence
of the indwelling Christ ?   Alas, alas, there is a
woeful discovery to be made by many when we
all come to be tried as by fire (1 Cor. iii.
13–15).

My dear brother, I cannot tell you how I feel
as I write these words—deep, deepening shame
and grief for myself, and vehement desires to have

Christ's work perfected in me.   May He in His abundant grace grant to you, and to me also (though most unfaithful and unworthy), the FULL EST MEASURES of what we have been meditating on, that are vouchsafed to souls in flesh.

CHAPTER XIX.

THE LORD JESUS.

WHAT was this Lord Jesus whom we so often hear and speak of? He was the Son of GOD, the Father's EQUAL; and He was also the Son of Man. Resting in His Father's bosom from Eternity, His heart was filled with boundless happiness, and this happiness came from one thing, ONLY ONE; He knew the Father and loved Him, and in turn was known and loved by His Father. To be short, let me just say that He would share this great joy of His with sinful and miserable men, all whose sin and misery came from two things: they did not know the Father, and what little they did know of Him they HATED (John xv. 24; xvi. 3). And so the SON of God became man that He might, in an intelligible way, reveal to men what GOD really is. And so the life and sufferings of Jesus are just the unseen heart of GOD made visible to us in the doings and the sayings of a man like ourselves, but without sin. And so, as we gaze on the lovely walk of Christ, we are to understand that in looking on Him we are looking ON THE FATHER (John xiv. 9). How precious is Christ's life in this aspect of it !

But, besides showing us what the Father is, Christ brought us a message from the Father—a message of LOVE. He brought to us an invitation to turn to GOD, with the assurance that He would welcome every returning prodigal with a kiss of loving forgiveness (Luke xv. 20). Nay, more, that He would make the returned sinner an actual SON, and love him with the very same love wherewith Christ Himself is loved (John xvii. 23).

But, besides this, the Lord Jesus had another commission. He was appointed, not only to reveal to us the Father, and to bring us that Message of love from the Father, but He was actually to BRING TO THE FATHER EVERY SOUL OF MAN THAT ACCEPTED THE INVITATION, AND WAS WILLING TO RETURN, for without this help of Christ the sinner's return would have been IMPOSSIBLE. But He, as the Good Shepherd, will pick up every lost sheep which is WILLING to be picked up, and laying it on His shoulders, will carry it home rejoicing (Luke xv. 5). Every difficulty He will overcome, for He is ABLE TO SAVE TO THE UTTER-MOST all that come unto God by Him (Heb. vii. 25). Let me here hint at three difficulties in the way. There is, first, the guilt of sin, and this the sinner could never put away. But the Lord Jesus has already taken it on Himself, and has died as a CURSE under it, and so the sinner who gives himself up to the Saviour is at once freely and fully forgiven. But, second, the sinner feels, "I do not love God." Well, I would reply, but Jesus can help you in this as in every other need. He can ACTUALLY MAKE YOU A NEW CREATURE, and this He does the moment you give yourself into His hands to have it done (2 Cor. v. 17). And though your love to God shall not be PERFECTED on earth, yet you shall love and obey Him in a way that shall be real and genuine, though it is sadly mingled with the defilements of your own fallen self-life. And then, when He takes you to heaven, the work shall be PERFECTED there, and you shall then love the Father and serve Him, as Jesus loves and serves. But there is a third difficulty. The sinner says, "It is a long road to heaven, and the road is crowded with deadly enemies and dangers of every kind. How can I ever cut my way through such a fierce and mighty army? There is the Devil and all his legions; there is the world, and everything in it; and, what is worst of all, there is my own flesh, my sin-loving and world-loving nature—and they are all determined that I shall never see heaven, if they can contrive to keep me out of it." To this I reply, Yes, beloved, it is all true; nay, it is less than the truth; nevertheless, greater is the Great Deliverer than all that can be against you. You are but a helpless lamb in a wilderness of ravening wolves; but the Good Shepherd, if you trust Him, will guard you by His mighty power, and none shall pluck you out of His hand (John x. 28).

CHAPTER XX.

CHRIST.

THE one grand object of adoring contemplation, whereby we may build up ourselves, is Christ (Eph. iii. 14 to end). The grand topic of brotherly communion is always Christ—Christ in His person, in His work, in His grace, in His glory, in His present intercession before the throne, in His expected return. Christ IN us, Christ ON us, Christ FOR us, but ever and only CHRIST. And we are strengthened to run our appointed race only as we look away from all besides to Jesus (Heb. xii. 1, 2). (The Greek word has the force of "away" in it.) "Preach Christ; all else is worthless," said a dying preacher of last century. "All out of Christ are but shadows," said the beloved Fletcher of Madeley. "If you would advance in all grace, STUDY CHRIST MUCH," says that holy man of God, Archbishop Leighton.

166

" *Christ* is EVERYTHING in Christianity," says John Wicliffe. And what less than this says the Psalmist : " Whom have I in heaven but Thee ? And there is none upon earth that I desire besides Thee."

And there is no fear that our most eager explorations will ever exhaust all that may be discovered in the breadth and length, the depth and height of His imperfectly-known, because unknowable, love. God's exceeding riches of grace are opened up to us in Him, for our present appropriation and enjoyment — and this up to our capacity to receive. There is no reserve held back from us; we are urged to receive until we be *filled* UP TO ALL THE FULNESS OF GOD (Eph. iii. 19). Such words, such thoughts, overpower the mind ; but they are the true sayings of God. They are the wine of the Kingdom (Song i. **2**, **4**), which He has provided for our trying journey, that such as be faint in the wilderness may drink (2 Sam. xvi. 2). Wherefore, let us give and take from each other fresh draughts of this wine when we are weary with the trials of the way, and are tempted to be " of heavy hearts " (Prov. xxxi. 6).

A beautiful word, a word " exceeding great and precious," spoken to us through the prophet Isaiah (chap. xxx. 18), has been echoing through my heart for many days past, like a strain of sweetest music. "Therefore will the Lord wait that He may be gracious unto you, and therefore will He be exalted, that He may have mercy upon you." Of course it was spoken to Israel ; but, removing from it what was merely dispensational, may we not take all these tender assurances of the Old Covenant, as well as all the promises, and count them our very own—all yea and amen TO US in Christ, our Head. And what a sweet and cheering thought underlies these words ! So far from grudging to give us any good thing (Ps. lxxxiv. 11), our God and Father waits patiently to do it. But why wait—why not give us at once ? No, it cannot be; no blessing would be really a blessing to us until we should be prepared to use it in a right and profitable way. Therefore, Divine love keeps the boon back till Divine wisdom sees that it would be safe and profitable to us to receive it. And how long has He been waiting ? In respect to certain blessings, or fuller measures of blessing, He has been waiting on us since our conversion—nay, longer, since our birth. *The moment* we are fit to receive, His opportunity for bestowing is come. Oh, let us seek, so far as the matter lies with us, to make that happy moment of higher, OF HIGHEST, blessing NOW (2 Cor. vi. 1, 2). Paul so lived (see Phil. iii. 12, 14), placing before the Lord every day a fresh opportunity for His bestowal on His faithful servant of fresh mercies. And the same God, "Rich in mercy," is as ready to deal with us all in the same "exceeding riches of His grace." There is never anything on the side of God to hinder His bestowal. Why should we permit any hindrance to remain on ours? I believe that many might, if faithful, grow as much *in a day* as they do in many years. May we have the faith that accepts the free gift of a WHOLE CHRIST, and HEARTILY YIELD UP TO THIS CHRIST OUR WHOLE AND ENTIRE SELVES (Rom. xii. 1).

CHAPTER XXI.

SONS OF GOD.

1. Now are we the Sons of God.

THIS subject is referred to in 1 John iii. 2—
"Beloved, now," or *already*, "are we the sons
of God." To be the very son of the Lord Almighty
(2 Cor. vi. 18), we can see at a glance, is the very
highest dignity possible to any creature ; so very
high that, in our present state, the honour and
blessedness of it are inconceivable. It all comes
out of the fact that the believer is made *one* with
Christ ; and so, because Christ is the *Son*, they who
receive Him share His *Sonship*, as they shall share
everything else which belongs to Him (John i. 12)·
Sonship belongs exclusively to the new creation.
There was no such thing, nor was there the
possibility of it, in the old creation. The old
creation is very comprehensive ; at the summit of
it stand the angels, and the line extended down to

the grain of dust; but nowhere within its wide circle is there such a being as a *child of God*.

It is most important that we see this clearly, that we may give Christ the high place in our hearts which belongs to Him. Even the angels are not *sons*. In Heb. i. 5 it is asked, "Unto which of the angels said He at any time, Thou art My Son?" No, at the highest, they are all—every one of them — ministering servants, who minister to the necessities of the true sons of God—even redeemed sinners (Heb. i. 14). This service they count a glorious honour. God has no son save the only-begotten, and believers who become sons only because they receive Christ as the incarnate Son of God. Had it not been for this, we would not have been sons any more than holy angels are, or than innocent Adam was. God never had any *sons* save Christ, and they who receive life through His name (John xx. 31).

We often hear of God as being the Father of all mankind. Now, I don't think this is true. Indeed, He loves all the race with a holy love, so deep, and free, and tender, as to have given His only-begotten *Son* to redeem us all; and He offers sonship to every one; but only they who accept Christ become sons. Alas, alas, the rest are as

Jesus said, " of your father the Devil." We are sons of God, then, not because we are His creatures and made in His image, but because we are born again, or from above. The sonship which is spoken of in the New Testament is quite unknown to the Old; for the time had not come for the full declaration of this matchless privilege. True, God speaks in the Prophets of His being a father to Israel, and He addresses them occasionally as children ; but on examining these passages, we find that, in every case, the words are strongly figurative. It is just as when He speaks of Himself as being a husband to Israel, and as married to their land (Isa. lxii.). These are plainly figures; and so too are the words which speak of Him as a father. But in the New Testament, the fatherhood and the sonship spoken of are not figures at all, but simple facts, to be understood according to the literal meaning of the words. God is as really the Father of every *regenerated* man and woman, as He is the Father of the Lord Jesus Christ.

The eternal Son, co-equal with the Father, was always the only-begotten Son. But when He became incarnate, and especially on His completion of the great work He had undertaken, He became *Son* under *new conditions*. It was AS GOD that

He had always been the *Son*, but now He became SON AS MAN. It was AS MAN that the Father bestowed on Him *all the glory* which He had eternally possessed AS GOD (see John xvii. 5). He is still, as He always was, Son AS GOD; but now He is also SON AS MAN. This is the name above every name which has been given Him in reward for His obedience unto death (Phil. ii. 6–9); this is the unequalled position to which He has been raised, far above principalities, and powers, and every name of dignity (Eph. i 21, 22) —viz., that the MAN Jesus Christ should be raised up to sit on the throne of God as God's co-equal Son. God, and yet A MAN—a man, and yet GOD; and, both as God and as man, the Son of God over all.

I desire that we should see very clearly that it is only through our reception by faith of Christ as the Son of God (John i. 12) that we can possibly reach this sonship, for it is only thus that we are born of God. But this marvellous relationship brings us inconceivably near to the Father. We are brought nearer to God by our new birth than the child is to its parents by its natural birth. Nay, we are nearer to Christ than even His mother Mary was by the bonds of motherhood, for Mary was nearer to Christ, much nearer, as a redeemed sinner, than

she was or could be as the mother of His sinless flesh.
Hence the way in which He speaks in Matt.
xii. 46–50. Nay, to say it all in a single word,
the Christian is, in a sense, as near to God and is as
really a child of God as the blessed Jesus is. He
and His people are led to the same glory (John
xvii. 22) by different ways—Jesus attained it by
Himself, we receive it from Him as the free gift of
His grace. No human religions, whether heathen,
or perverted Jewish, or perverted Gospel, ever
hinted at the exceeding riches of Divine grace as
being on a scale so immense as this. Even in the
Old Testament, God's obedient ones are spoken of
as *servants*, but not as SONS. That dispensation
was not prepared for the full light of this wonderful
truth. Till after Christ the revelation of this truth
would not have been intelligible; and till the
coming of the Holy Ghost it would have been
grievously abused.

While none but those who truly believe that
Jesus is the Son of God enjoy this privilege, *all*
who thus believe do. Many of them may not be
conscious of the fact that sonship is theirs—still, it
is theirs. The baby born yesterday is as really the
child of its father, and is as tenderly beloved, as the
grown-up son ; and in God's family there are little

babes, and children at all stages of advance. The very little ones scarcely know what they are; but the Father knows them and loves them all. No earthly father loves his children as God loves His; and if an earthly father could not despise or neglect his infant because it is so ignorant and helpless, infinitely less will God do so. Oh, let us never forget that "as a father pitieth his children, so the Lord pitieth them that fear Him." And when we think of His *Father-love*, let us put far more meaning into the word than we could when we speak of earthly father-love, as the infinite God Himself is above puny man.

The little ones are ofttimes distressed with the fear that they have lost this sonship, because they have lost the joy of it. And they are especially troubled with this fear when they see the workings of corruption within their hearts. Their feeble faith can scarcely retain its confidence when it looks a little deeper into the bottomless depths of their own depravity; and they cannot believe that creatures so unworthy can possibly be children of God. But the faith of these, though strong enough to bring them truly into sonship, is not ample enough to keep them in the comfort of it. They were not taken into the family of God because they were *worthy* of the honour (no holiest angel is worthy), but because they had accepted Christ; and Christ is *so worthy,* that for His sake *alone,* all who receive Him are made sons and daughters of the Lord Almighty. And as their own worthiness did not place them in the Father's bosom as His children, so neither can the want of it keep any out, or turn any out. All our worthiness lies in our having received *God's Son;* and this every true believer *has,* and every sinner may have, so soon as he accepts it on God's own terms. But this tendency to be dejected because of felt unworthiness, comes out of a degree of legalism and self-righteousness, which the person who is afflicted with it should watch and pray against.

May our God and Father enable us to walk worthy of the wonderful grace which He has bestowed on us, in making us the very children of His infinite love, and the heirs along with Christ of His kingdom and glory.

2. FAITH'S PRESENT ENJOYMENT OF SONSHIP.

I AM glad that you enter into my remarks about the infinite grace of God in bestowing upon believers the unequalled privilege of being sons of the Lord Almighty. Perhaps we cannot do better than continue the subject in this letter, and may the Holy Spirit open up to our understandings the marvellous truth, and also apply it with power to our hearts.

This inconceivable privilege is not merely a matter of future hope, but it is designed for faith's present enjoyment. Now are we the sons of God, and this not the less that the sonship is not as yet visibly manifested (1 John iii. 2). In fact, just as in the case of Jesus His sonship was concealed from all but spiritual eyes, so in the case of believers only spiritual eyes can discern the faintest trace of this sonship. They are poor, and despised, and are sometimes counted the filth of the world and the offscouring of all things (1 Cor. iv. 13).

But God recognises this wonderful relationship, Christ recognises it, the Holy Spirit recognises it, nay, one of His chief operations in our hearts is to keep up in us the continual recognition of it, for

2:12

He incites in us the believing cry of "ABBA, FATHER!" (Gal. iv. 6). Let us then humbly, joyously recognise our true relationship to God as OUR VERY FATHER in Christ Jesus, for we need the strength for holy living, which the firm faith of it can alone supply us with. It is not lowly humility which shrinks from recognising it; it is legalism and the self-righteousness which springs from unbelief.

This matchless privilege involves all the blessedness which God can give us, since He has made us His very children; after that, what good thing shall He, or can He, grudge to give us? But this sonship equally involves, on our side, all the devoted obedience which it is in the power of regenerated men to render. Let us seek grace, therefore, to accept all that our FATHER gives us— refusing nothing. In both of these respects, the Lord Jesus is our perfect example. He accepted everything that the Father gave Him. He rendered everything He had, even His life, at the will of His Father. How perfectly groundless, when looked at in the light of sonship, are the fears of the believer that God may, perhaps, leave him unprovided for; it is IMPOSSIBLE. He is counted an unusually wicked father who could leave his helpless infants to starve, and shall God's children

think of Him as being a Father after that fashion ?
No ; let us show our faith in our Father's love by
our courageous trust in Him, however we may be
placed. "None perish that Him trust." Rather
than forsake a single child of His in desolation, He
would send a legion of angels with plentiful supplies
to him. The simple truth is, that God cares just as
tenderly for every child of His, as He cared for His
only-begotten co-equal Son while He tabernacled
on earth. Not one hair of our head can perish,
for He keeps loving count of their number. If we
believe all this as a doctrine, we must show it by
our practice. We must cast ALL our care on Him,
knowing that He careth for us. There is nothing
by means of which the great destroyer works more
havoc to the souls of God's children than by those
crowds of unbelieving cares and worldly anxieties,
which are so dishonouring to God and so hurtful to
ourselves (1 Peter v. 7, 8).

3. BROTHERHOOD OF ALL THE CHILDREN
OF GOD.

WE must not forget that this greatest privilege
of sonship with God brings with it a second

privilege—brotherhood with all the children of
God. If God be our Father, then, as a matter
of course, every child of God must be our brother
or our sister.

I have termed this relationship a privilege, and
every truly spiritual mind will feel it to be such;
but to the fleshly, selfish man, however religious
he may be, it will seem to be an oppressive burden.
But the same genuine faith which accepts with
glad heart and free the wondrous truth of God's
fatherhood, receives also with joy the kindred
truth of the brotherhood of all the redeemed. If
we do not recognise in that poor but pious man
or woman, with mean garb and unfashionable
manners, a brother or a sister on whom our hearts
delight to rest in love, we have no right to look up
and call God our FATHER. The same Divine
Word which reveals the one truth equally reveals
the other; the same genuine faith which heartily
accepts the one, accepts both; and the same Spirit
who works in us to cry, "Abba, Father," works in
us to feel a brother's love for all whom we recognise as being the Father's children. "For he that
loveth not his brother, whom he hath seen, cannot
love God whom he hath not seen" (1 John iv.
20, *R.V.*).

4. Our walk as Children of God.

Since God has made us His children, how responsible we are to glorify our Father by living so as to please Him. We are to be "blameless and harmless, children of God, without blemish, in the midst of a crooked and perverse generation," among whom we are called to shine, especially by our conduct, " as LIGHTS in the world " (Phil. ii. 15). Having the spirit of Christ, and actually LED by that spirit, our conduct will not resemble, but will contrast with, the conduct of those who are not children of God, but filled with enmity to Him, and who are guided by that spirit which now worketh in the children of disobedience. Nay, our present walk, as children of God, should not only contrast with that of the world, but it should contrast equally with our own past selves. Once DARKNESS, we are now LIGHT ; and are meant to walk as CHILDREN of the LIGHT (Eph. v. 8). What a difference—midnight darkness and broad daylight ! Light amid surrounding darkness—a lily among thorns, a lamb among wolves. . . . Such the child of God is always to be. The sons of God are to be like their Father, and it is only by their being so that they shall fulfil their mission

in the world.   And, in seeking to discharge our
mission, it is to be in the full, free, and joyous
spirit of sons, and not as bond-slaves.

---

5. OUR SERVICE AS CHILDREN OF GOD.

I HAVE already said that in seeking to discharge
our mission as the children of God, our obedience is
to be in the free and joyous spirit of sons, and not
as bond-slaves.   It is not that we do certain
appointed acts, but that we do them from love.
You would not think highly of the spirit of a
servant who did all his work merely for sake of
the wages; and I don't think the spirit of a professed Christian a whit different, who is religious
for sake of the heaven which he expects to reach
by it—the one is just as selfish as the other.
No ; whatever is not done in LOVE is not accepted
(see 1 Cor. xiii. 1–3).   Our aim should be to do
as much service to our Father as we can, and in
the doing of it to please Him perfectly.   The aim
of the slave is that he gets his task done, lest he
should be punished; and the aim of the hireling is,
to secure the hire ; and *he* is none the less a slave,
or a hireling, who attempts to serve God only lest

he should be punished in hell, or for the sake of attaining heaven. Those who have the spirit of sonship serve in the joyous spirit of devoted love. They were delivered from condemnation, and were declared heirs of the Kingdom from the moment that they became ONE with Christ ; and they serve God, not for selfish ends of their own, but because they love God, who is their Father in Christ ; and His approving smile is to them a joy unspeakable and full of glory. And having such a FATHER, how devoted should our service be.

There is no kind of service known among men which is so delightful as that of a loving child ; compared with it a hireling's, who works for money, or a slave's, who merely dreads the lash, is nothing. And I do not think it would be pressing the analogy too far to affirm that no service which is rendered to God by any creature, even by angels, is so delightful to Him as that of a redeemed sinner whom, in His grace, He has made His own child in Christ Jesus. Oh, let us seek with earnest prayer and ceaseless watchfulness to serve Him as His loving children ! and though our department of service be lowly and obscure, let our discharge of it be in PURE LOVE. The earlier years of our Lord's life were spent in a very lowly ministry of obedient love to His Father, in a carpenter's shop; and we may be sure of it that He worked as faithfully, and as lovingly, as when at His Father's bidding He went forth to preach the Gospel to the poor, to cleanse lepers, and to raise the dead. And God is to be served in no other spirit than that of devoted, self-sacrificing, child-like love. They that are in the flesh cannot please God.

Since God is our Father, these two things at least are sure to follow—First, That He shall be sure to care for us, and keep us, and, in every case, to do for us the very best that is possible. Can such a Father neglect His child? It were blasphemy to think it; it is wickedness to fear it. "He cannot deny Himself." Second, Having such a Father, how should we comport ourselves towards Him? What love, what trust, what obedience, what resignation, what utter ABANDONMENT of ourselves into His trusted hands! And, when we fail in these, what lowly confessions, what penitential sorrow should there be, and what earnest, importunate prayer for help to enable us to live as becomes the children of such a Father—and a prayer like this shall always be answered.

CHAPTER XXII.

THE FELLOWSHIP OF GOD'S SON.

1. ONE LIFE.

WHAT an amazing word is that in 1 Cor. i. 9. We are called to the FELLOWSHIP of the SON OF GOD. Try to think as clearly as you can of what is meant by this word FELLOWSHIP. The nearest approach to a perfect fellowship which we have on earth, is that which subsists between a most affectionate husband and wife, when heart is knit to heart, as God meant them to be. They have every earthly possession, and enjoyment, in COMMON. What belongs to one belongs to both. Their interests are identical, their children are the children of both, their home belongs equally to each—but this is the merest shadow of the infinitely more intimate FELLOWSHIP between Christ and every believing soul. The two are ONE SPIRIT; which husband and wife cannot be (1 Cor. vi. 17).

185

The one lives within the other; and He thinks
and feels, speaks and acts, through the other
(Gal. ii. 20; Phil. i. 21). What union between
husband and wife approaches this? In fact, Christ
and His people have only one life between them,
for He is their life; as for their old life, it is to be
counted DEAD (Col. iii. 3). His Father is now our
Father (John i. 12; xx. 17); His home is our
home (John xvii. 24); His glory He shares with
us (John xvii. 22); He seats His people with Him
on His very *throne* (Rev. v. 9, 10). He keeps
back NOTHING, but all that the Father gave Him
He opens up to us to make present use of, so far
as we are spiritually able to appropriate and enjoy
it. The same love of the same Infinite Father,
which rests on Jesus with ineffable delight, rests
this day on ourselves (John xvii. 26); and let us
remember that it is just because our Father so
loves us that He so chastens us. The same wisdom which arranged the life of Jesus and guided
His steps, is now arranging our lot and is guiding
us continually; while the same Omnipotent Arm is
beneath us and around us.

2. ONE INTEREST.

LET us read 1 Cor. i. 9 as setting before us what the Gospel, in the spirit of it, really is. It is not a demand on God's part that we who are dead in sin should *do* such and such things, or *be* so and so, ere He consent to be favourable unto us; but it is a *call* on God's part that we, utterly ruined sinners, should enter into fellowship with His beloved Son. It is the outcome of God's love and mercy, of that God who is " rich in mercy " (Eph. ii. 4); nay, it is " the exceeding riches of His grace " (verse 7). And all this is done for us " even when we were dead in sins; " so far are we from deserving any favour. And so intimate is the UNION with Christ which this fellowship involves, that virtually we believers already share Christ's very life, have been raised with Him in His resurrection, and are seated with Him on His throne. All this VIRTUALLY. The Gospel is God's call to a lost sinner to enter into and to enjoy all this; and saving faith is the hearty acceptance of the invitation and response to the call (1 Cor. i. 9). After we accept this call, we may count on God's *faithfulness* to carry out all that the call holds out to us. In other words, that God will look upon us, and deal with us, as creatures who are in the closest conceivable union with His beloved Son.

Now, from all this, let us draw this important practical rule : Since God NEVER forgets our perfect ONENESS with Christ, let us also ALWAYS keep it in mind ; and let us never think of ourselves at all apart from the Lord Jesus. Never. In fact, we have no such self at all to think about, for our old cursed, Christless self has been brought to a final end, crucified with Christ (Gal. ii. 20). And so, when we look at self, let us look at self IN CHRIST, as " accepted in the Beloved," adopted to be children of God in Him. When we search out our sins (and we ought to do so) let us look at them as sins in which Christ is as deeply concerned as we are ; sins which have been laid on His head, and for the cleansing of which His blood has been already shed and already accepted. When we realise our weakness and our wants (and oh, how weak and how empty we are !) let us equally think of Christ's fulness (Col. i. 19). And let us remember that the fulness is just as much ours as the want is, because of this wonderful fellowship. When we think of our duties, let us not think of them apart from Him. They are duties which He is ready to help us to discharge, for He has undertaken to do so. And when we think of our terrible enemies, let us look on them as Christ's enemies quite as much as they are ours; enemies, moreover, that He has a keen eye upon, and a strong hand stretched out over ; enemies that He has already met and struggled with, and vanquished—met and vanquished on our behalf. And having bruised them under His own feet, He will never rest till He crushes them beneath ours (Rom. xvi. 20).

What wonderful truths are these ! Oh, may everything send us in renewed faith, desire, joy, and love to Him our head ; apart from whom we have nothing at all, but in whom we have everything that can enrich the creature. The Lord lead us into the deep experience of all His wonderful grace in Christ Jesus.

___

3. UNION AND ONENESS.

I HAVE just been reading in John xv. our Lord's wonderful parable of the vine and its branches, and which also sets before us the blessed truth that Christ and His people are ONE. This union is so close that all figures fail to set it forth worthily. It is compared to the union between the head and the members, which together form one body. We are said to be members of His body, of His flesh, and of His bones (Eph. v. 30). It is compared to the union between husband and wife ; and here, to that between a tree and its branches. But all these figures fall short of the astonishing truth, that He dwelleth in us and we dwell in Him (John vi. 56). There is no union among creatures to which it can be suitably compared, and there is no union in the universe which equals it, saving the union in the Adorable Trinity, of Father, Son, and Holy Ghost.

How frequent in the Epistles is the expression " IN CHRIST," sometimes varied under the form of " CHRIST IN US"; but I fear these expressions, brimful of infinite wealth of meaning, are read very lightly, as if they spoke merely of a Christian profession. They express this ONENESS, that the believing sinner, who alone is warranted to appropriate them, is really and is inseparably ONE with the Incarnate Son of God, as the Son is really and inseparably ONE with the Father. Only think of it— if we be truly believing in Christ, He is closer to us, INFINITELY CLOSER, and more INTIMATELY united to us, than our own soul is to our body, for He is our very life.

By this union, Christ, and all the fulness of God which is in Him, becomes ours (Col. ii. 9), while

we, and all that we are, or have, become absolutely
His own for ever. He keeps nothing back from
us, but shares all ; we are to keep nothing back
from Him, but trustingly, joyfully surrender all
into His hands. Our substance, our powers of
mind and body, our health, our life—we are to
give up everything to His disposal. We have no
longer anything which self can count its own. We
must take tremulous heed not to delude ourselves
with the common, but most unscriptural, notion
that faith consists in the believing of certain ortho-
dox doctrines, based upon certain proof-texts. No,
indeed ; if this be all that the man has, the belief
of the multiplication-table will do him nearly as
much good. Faith is that act in which the man
CHOOSES to accept Christ, and to give himself up to
Christ, on Christ's own terms, and to enter into
this everlasting oneness with Him. And the life
of faith which follows on this first great act of faith,
is a continual recognition of this wondrous union,
SO AS TO LIVE IN THE POWER OF IT. The man, in
conscious emptiness and helplessness in himself,
counts the fulness of Christ to be accessible to
him for supply of every need ; and so he goes in
faith to Him for everything he wants. And he
equally realises that he is now not his own, but is

the willing organ of the indwelling Christ ; and so he yields himself up to Christ's use of him in such a way that it is not himself merely who thinks, and feels, and speaks, and acts, but it is also Christ, who dwelleth in him.   This life of the man and the life of Christ within him are not two lives, but one (see Gal. ii. 20).

This marvellous ONENESS is effected by a vigorous act of will on both sides.   The Lord Jesus CHOOSES with all His heart to be ONE with the consenting sinner ; while the sinner CHOOSES with all his heart to be one with Him.   We may liken it, in a way, to the marriage union, which is similarly formed by mutual consent.   It is asked : " Do you take this woman to be your wife ? "   The answer is : " I do."   " Do you take this man for your husband ? "   " I do."   And this constitutes the marriage.   And faith is neither more nor less than the soul's hearty consent to enter into union with Christ ON HIS OWN TERMS.

How solemn, how tenderly touching, it is to think that the Son of God, in His LOVE to us, has chosen to be thus MADE ETERNALLY ONE with us ! He has passed by angels, and has set His whole heart, not only on dust and ashes like us, but on creatures who, when we saw Him, hated Him, and

MURDERED HIM. On the other hand, we, in our love to Him, have gladly forsaken all that we had, hating for His sake even our own life. Heaven is the world of love; but even in heaven there is no love known like that of Christ for His bride; and on earth there is no love can match with the love of the saint for His Saviour. Just now we are most unlike Him, unworthy of being seen beside Him, but in due time He shall make every unit of His own "perfect in beauty," and worthy of being seen at His side as His companion for evermore.

Oh, what a powerful motive have we in all this to constrain us to look on sin with horror! I am often touched by a common and most expressive figure used in the Old Testament to set forth how intolerably loathsome to God are the sins of His people. It is spoken of as adultery (see Ezek. xvi. and elsewhere). A pure-minded, chaste, and loving wife would rather be flung to wild beasts than tolerate the bare thought of unfaithfulness to a loving and beloved husband. And the Christian's dread of any sin whatever should go far beyond this.

The actual bond of union is the Holy Spirit who dwells both in Christ and in all His members.

2:13

Christ gives Him to be our guide, our strength, our very life; and we receive Him, and subject ourselves to His absolute control. "If any man have not the spirit of Christ he is none of His"; and it is they, and they alone, who are led by the spirit of God who are the sons of God (Rom. viii. 9, 14).

What wonderful things are these on which we have been trying to muse! Oh, may the Lord help us to live in the humble joy, and strength, and unreserved devotedness, which a firm faith in them cannot fail to give—never let us think of ourselves apart from Him. We are not our own, we are Christ's own, and are one with Him. There is no one has any interest in us like Christ's interest. Let us leave Him to consult only His own interest in us; and when He does so, He is doing the best that can be done to secure our highest interests of every kind—since His interest and ours are not now separate, but identical, and that for ever.

---

4. "WE ARE NOT OUR OWN."

We never were our own. For God made us to be His — made us out of nothing, and has all along fed us and sustained us—nay, though we rebelled against Him, and set up to live as our own, He never, never for a moment, gave up His claim upon us.   And now He has added a new and a most wonderful ground of claim to us, He has *redeemed us to be His.*   And He has paid for us, oh, what a price!   And now this last claim on us is stronger than all that went before.

And we are wholly God's own—our bodies and our souls, and all that belongs to both.   Our health, our possessions, our faculties, all are given to us that, as belonging *only* to God, we may devote them all to His glory.

Oh, what a sweet, sweet thought it is for a poor, desolate, worthless, sinful worm to think : *I belong to the Lord Jesus.*   I am His as nothing else in heaven or in earth is His—I am His peculiar possession.   For we are altogether His, and His alone ; His to love Him with all our hearts ; His to lay our very persons in living sacrifice upon His altar (Rom. xii. 1).   We are His to the inconceivable extent that our very sins were made His, and He was made answerable for them, even to death ; while His righteousness makes us who *are His* righteous in Him (2 Cor. v. 21).   We are so really His that He lives in us (Gal. ii. 20), for if we be truly His, it is not our own life but His that now carries on our daily living ; and the affections that now glow in our regenerated hearts are the movements of the very bowels of Jesus Christ (Phil. i. 8). And we have nothing any longer that belongs to us ; He claimed us as His, with all that we had, and we resigned ourselves with all our belongings into His trusted and beloved hands. And now all that concerns us lies with Him (Ps. xxxi. 15). We choose nothing, we seek to escape nothing ; but we leave to Him to appoint for us just what He pleases, and we welcome His appointment. The cup which He mixes for us, and blesses as He puts it into our hands, we meekly drink (John xviii. 11). What once caused us care we no longer trouble ourselves about, but we cast all our care on Him, since we belong to Him (1 Peter v. 7). Fierce conflicts often assail us, but the battle is not ours, it is His (2 Chron. xx. 15). And we fight it only with His weapons, and look with confidence to share in His victory (Rom. viii. 37). Whether He prefer that we shall be weak or strong, be blind or seeing, be in desolate poverty or in outward comfort, all is alike to us, since we belong eternally to Him.

5. No Secrets between us.

WE should pray and strive that, as the days go past with us, every day may find Christ a little bit higher in our hearts than He was the day before. Let us live FOR Jesus. Let us live ON Jesus, and on Jesus ONLY. The blessed life is the life which is lived in Enoch-like walking with Him, leaning on Him, conversing with Him, opening up all our hearts to Him, and listening, with ravishing delight, as by His Word and Spirit He opens up all His heart to us. Let there be no secrets between us. Let us tell Him everything; tell Him all our joys and our sorrows, our hopes and fears, our desires and our perplexities—and be sure we tell Him our SINS. Let there be only ONE will between us, and let that will be HIS. Never, NEVER let us use our own will at all, except to say AMEN to His. And consult Him about everything—our small matters as well as our great, our temporal and our eternal interests. Never for an instant forget that we are inconceivably DEAR TO HIM, the very apple of His eye; that He has given to us HIS WHOLE UNDIVIDED HEART, and will not, cannot, be satisfied with anything less than our WHOLE UNDIVIDED HEART in return. In other words, He gives Himself ALL to us, and He wants us to take Him, and use Him, and rejoice in Him, as our EVERYTHING. And this means that we have nothing else besides. The Lord strengthen us, beloved, to live in this spirit, with increasing singleness of eye.

CHAPTER XXIII.

DIVINE COMPENSATIONS.

I UNDERSTAND " Compensation " to mean a something on the *one side* that goes to counter-balance a *corresponding something* on the *other*. Your friend, I dare say, uses the term with reference to the outward circumstances of a man's lot in life, and to the DOUBLE influence which each of these circumstances exerts on his spiritual interests. The FAVOURABLE circumstances (or what are counted such) are not *altogether* favourable, but have compensating drawbacks ; while the UNFAVOURABLE circumstances are not altogether unfavourable, but have compensating advantages. It is the part of wisdom, then, to look at the entire set of circumstances amid which God has set us, as a perfectly adjusted whole, and to lie passive in His gracious hands, saying " *Amen* " to His sovereign disposal of us.

In fact there are no circumstances in a Christian's lot that can rightly be spoken of as *evil*. For that lot, down to its minutest details, is all arranged by God ; and " as for God, HIS way is *perfect* " (Ps. xviii. 30); perfect in its wisdom as in its love. He has devised a wonderful plan in regard to each of us, and He is working it out daily and hourly with persevering steadfastness. But we too, alas, allow ourselves to form plans about our own lives; and, as His plan and ours, about ourselves, are never the same, the working out of His plan is certain to cross ours at a thousand points. These points, where *our* plan is marred by *His*, we call EVILS ; and this subject of " compensation " may be useful to us if our meditation on it helps us to feel more deeply that any circumstance may become good when God is pleased to use it for our good, and that any circumstance may be made an evil to us, if in self-will we seek to enjoy it, or employ it, apart from God, and for our own ends.

The circumstances of a man's life may be roughly grouped into two classes, the pleasant and the unpleasant. The pleasant things in our lot we easily see to be mercies; and we are thankful for them. This is so far right, but these pleasant things are also trials, and full of danger to us; and we have need, in enjoying them, to cry "Lead us not into temptation." For their helpfulness has a perilous "compensation" annexed to it. Good health, for instance, and kind friends, and worldly comforts are very pleasant, and they are God's good gifts. But how often, I had almost said how invariably, are they more or less misused. How many sinners do they keep lying like besotted drunkards, asleep in the arms of the wicked one (1 John v. 19, *R.V.*). Aye, and how many Christians are feeble and languid, living and little more than living, because of their enjoyment of these mercies. The prodigal in Luke xv. would never have sought his father had he found rest in the "far country." Israel would never have sought God in penitence, if He had not planted thick hedges with sharp thorns between her and her former enjoyments (Hosea ii. 6, 7). No one ever seeks God, except under the pressure of constraining need. It is for this that affliction is sent. On the other hand, the natural effect of outward ease is Godless worldliness (see Ps. lxxiii. ; and mark the word " THEREFORE " in verse 6). " THEREFORE pride compasseth them about as a chain ; violence covereth them as a garment."

On the other hand, outward trial is unpleasant,

and it is not to be desired for its own sake. " Now
no chastening for the present seemeth to be joyous,
but grievous : nevertheless afterward it yieldeth the
peaceable fruit of righteousness unto them which
are exercised thereby " (Heb. xii. 11). Thus its
issues are, with God's blessing, VERY PRECIOUS, and
this is its " *compensation* " : it worketh the peaceable fruits of righteousness ; and as the results of
its precious efficacy stretch forward into eternity, it
enriches the soul that is suitably exercised by it,
infinitely beyond the calculation of angelic intellect.
We are told again, " that our light affliction, which
is but for a moment, worketh for us a far more
exceeding and eternal weight of glory " (2 Cor.
iv. 17). Note in this verse that the affliction is
spoken of as actually WORKING OUT the glory, so
that the same degree of glory would not be reached
apart from the affliction.

Without being made truly HUMBLE, no man shall
ever be EXALTED. " For every one that exalteth
himself shall be abased ; and he that humbleth himself shall be exalted " (Luke xviii. 14). Humility
is to be regarded as an indispensable prerequisite
for the everlasting glory. No man, unless he be
" poor in spirit," can expect to inherit the eternal
kingdom (Matt. v. 3). Now, there are two

influences that are needed to work in man this indispensable humility. He must be placed in circumstances which are more or less humiliating. There is a positive "need be" for this; and therefore the Lord never omits this mode of treatment in the training of His best-beloved children (Jas. ii. 5; Heb. xii. 6–10; Rev. iii. 19). Affliction is merely another word for these humiliating circumstances; and besides these, the man needs, also, the gracious operation of the Holy Spirit on his heart, to render efficacious all these external instrumentalities. But the whole process is carried on in a love that is unutterable; and the issues aimed at are so glorious, that even now, amid our severest trials, we should be able, not only to rejoice exceedingly, but to rejoice with a joy that is unspeakable, in the liveliest anticipations of the glorious outcome (1 Pet. i. 6–8, 13).

The principle to which we are referring, is just as applicable to the believer's SERVICE, as it is to his spiritual development and his training for eternal glory. Perhaps you have read a little book of last century, "Frazer on Sanctification." The writer of it had one of the most unsuitable wives that ever afflicted a good man; but the sore trial was useful to refine and elevate his spirit, and without the wife he would never have been able to write the book.

Next to our actual salvation, we should set our hearts on God's use of us. Like the prophet, so soon as we have been purged ourselves we should cry, " Here am I, send me " (Isa. vi. 8). But if God use us, He will do it in a sphere of His own choosing, and not of ours ; and He will do it in a way that carries out His own plans, and not ours. And these plans of His are sure to thwart and upset our own. But if we be observant, we shall see, long ere all be done, that there have been blessed compensations in our lot, nay, when all is done we shall see that these compensations, so called, have been not even " compensations," that there was no evil in our lot to be compensated, that, in short, God's way with us, from first to last, has been ALTOGETHER " A RIGHT WAY."

John Bunyan, for instance, lay in Bedford jail for more than a dozen years. His earnest voice was stilled ; and he who, of all men in England of that day, was one of the best fitted to exhibit clearly the rich grace of God to sinful men, was not allowed to speak at all. "What a pity!" said some. " What a mystery ! " said others. It was neither a pity nor yet a mystery; it was God's grand plan for Bunyan's more fruitful ministry. In his prison he wrote "The Pilgrim's Progress," a book that has been many times more useful to the Church than all his preaching could have been, and which would not have been written had he not been confined. What a "*compensation*," as it is called.

And similarly we might glance at Paul's imprisonment at Rome. He had there to confine his ministry to a very narrow sphere indeed. The caged eagle could leap only from spar to spar of his narrow cage. But his epistles—he wrote the warmest and the profoundest of them there—have been a more blessed service, *on the whole*, than his living voice could have been.

And glance, too, at Paul's early training for his subsequent ministry. In his pharisaic days see his legal self-righteous zeal. It knew no limits. It set him even on bloodthirsty persecution. What a pity! Nay, no pity at all. The suffering martyrs were not injured a bit, for God gave them blessed "compensation" through their sufferings; while Paul himself was learning the utter worthlessness of Judaism, and was being fitted to become, when God's set time should come, the Apostle of the Gentiles.

Let me remind you, too, of the devout Jonathan

Edwards. He was most ungratefully treated by his people at Northampton. They drove him away. As men speak, his prospects were ruined. No, he was simply set at leisure to write these books which have multiplied his serviceableness a hundredfold.

We have glanced at this subject of Divine compensations in its bearing on our spiritual education, and also in its bearing on a Christian's service to the Lord ; but even in regard to a believer's present joy (a very subordinate matter) these Divine compensations are very wonderful. In July, 1856, I sat beside the dying bed of one who had been a sorely-afflicted saint. He had had twelve children, and they all had been taken from him ; his wife had also been taken, and he was very poor. He said to me one morning, with a bright face : " I have got wonderful light last night on God's dealings with me. He has been kind, kind, and yet so blind have I been that I never saw it till now. I felt that He had sorely afflicted me in taking away all my beloved ones, and though I bowed under His holy hand, yet I felt it to be a sore trial. But I see His goodness in it now. *Every one of my children is in glory*, and I am going to join them. How anxious would I have been this day, if I had to leave them in a world like this. But they are all safe with the

Lord, and I want nothing more. My heart is full of thankfulness, for the Lord has taken them all." Was this no " compensation " ? Alas, that his faith in God had not been simple enough to have put him in possession of this peace and joy many years before his triumphant end. How many a tear would it have spared him—how many a song of praise would it have enabled him to sing !

In fact, we allow ourselves to reason far too much in regard to spiritual matters; while we trust in God, with entire singleness of heart, far too little. The injury thus done to ourselves is inconceivable. Our entire blessedness comes to us only as we exercise this simple faith. And since God is what we believe Him to be—infinite in every adorable perfection—how safely may we trust Him ; at the same time, our trust must necessarily be exercised in the dark, must be trust in GOD HIMSELF, without any adequate comprehension of His plans regarding us. We see from the Old Testament, and from our Lord's own words, that God the Father had a minutely-detailed life-plan for His beloved Son. He has a life-plan for every child of His, which is equally minute. Let us, therefore, seek to imitate the example of our Lord, and judge not after the sight of our eyes (Isa. xi. 3) ; but, whatever our

outward lot may be, to trust in the Lord with our
whole heart and lean not unto our own understanding (Prov. iii. 5), and be always ready to exclaim
with joy : " Though I be poor and needy, yet the
Lord is planning for me " (Ps. xl. 17).

CHAPTER XXIV.

TAUGHT OF GOD.

1. The insufficiency of Man's Teaching.

WHERE and how are we to get this teaching of God? I know no way but to get it from GOD alone. Paul had been long taught of man. He had sat at the feet of the great teachers of his day, and he had profited to appearance by their teaching above most of his fellows (Gal. i. 14). But what was it all worth? Why, only this—it made him the greater Pharisee; and we may also sit at the feet of the famous teachers in our day, but, if that be all, we shall be sure to profit as little. Let us see how Paul got his right teaching at last, for we must get it in the same way.

Please to read Gal. i. 15, 16, and note these points—First, Paul's present teaching was by REVELATION. See, too, Eph. i. 17, 18, and carefully notice, from 1 Cor. ii. 10–14, that no teaching except this alone is worth anything.　But EVERY ONE of GOD'S children gets this teaching (see John vi. 45). Second, This revelation was made to the man himself, and it was made DIRECTLY by GOD.　It was not a something that some Gamaliel taught, or even something that some old prophet had said ; but it was a distinct and direct revelation made by GOD to Paul himself.　There is a general revelation which is made to all in the written Word ; but, though in its own place it is indispensable, it is in no case sufficient.　Paul had the Old Testament revelation, and see what he made of it.　And without this special revelation of Christ to the soul, you and I shall make just as poor a use of the NEW. In Matt. xi. 27 our Lord affirms the necessity of this internal revelation ; without it the revelation made to us in the Word will be misused by us, but this special teaching secures the end designed.　Third, This revelation made to Paul, which changed him into an entirely new man, was not a statement of any doctrines, or an explanation of doctrine, it was an actual revelation of CHRIST in His glory.　As he says, GOD revealed His SON in me. (See the story in Acts ix.)　Alas, that in our day we make so much of doctrines, and so LITTLE, so very LITTLE, of Christ. It is this and that doctrine that they preach, and they think that all will be right if we believe their doctrine. No, we must have Christ Himself revealed by the Father in us, and continuing to live within us, and work all our works (see Gal. ii. 20).

There are three ways then in which men may acquire Divine truth. We may get it from man, as Paul did in his early days. Then there is the better way of going to God for light, and seeking to gather up what He has revealed to us in His holy Word. This is the best we can do of ourselves, but though it may give us much important information about God, it cannot reveal to us GOD Himself. We are still ignorant of God, and must remain so until the SON reveal Him (Matt. xi. 27). It is this last that is saving. But if we be faithful in searching the Word in order that we may truly learn the will of GOD, and if we set ourselves, in an "honest and good heart," to obey that will as we discover it, then GOD shall most assuredly meet us, and shall reveal Himself to us in such ways as He never fails to do to EVERY sincerely seeking soul. He shall fulfil to us the magnificent words spoken in 1 John ii. 20, 27. In this way do we come to KNOW the only true GOD and His CHRIST, in which knowledge lies the ETERNAL LIFE (see John xvii. 3).

The Lord Jesus once asked the twelve what the people said of Him. They answered that the people were divided in their opinions about Him (see Matt. xvi. 13), and notice that, among all these different opinions, there was none that took Him to be what He really was—the SON of GOD. They were all busy thinking about Him, and all talking about Him, but they were all wrong. And why were they all wrong ? We shall see immediately. He then asked, But what do *you* take Me to be ? In the name of the rest Peter replied, "Thou art the CHRIST, the SON of the living GOD." Jesus accepted the confession, commended the confessor, and ascribed his discovery of the fact to the direct REVELATION of the FATHER : "Flesh and blood hath not revealed it unto thee, but My Father which is in heaven."

---

2. SITTING AT THE FEET OF JESUS.

HE who would be taught aright MUST go to the LORD JESUS Himself for His teaching, and must sit, like MARY, at the feet of the saint's only Master.

Every saved soul is taught of GOD (John vi. 45).

Oh, what an infinite distance between being taught of GOD and taught only by man ! Man's teaching may fill the head plentifully with clear notions, but GOD's teaching enriches, gladdens, and sanctifies the heart. We may enjoy the very best teaching which man can give us, while we remain quite unable to profit by the lesson ; but God's teaching is always efficacious. He teacheth savingly and to profit. Every man that has learned of the FATHER, actually cometh to Jesus, but no others come (John vi. 45).

And the great lesson we have got to learn is CHRIST (see Eph. iv. 20), and we have no other teacher to teach it (see verse 21). And everything CHRIST teaches us about Himself is unspeakably precious ; though the most precious part of the lesson is that which sets before us CHRIST'S own internal life, and how we too may be made partakers of it. This highest of all lessons we increasingly learn as our own inner life becomes more like His, or, in other words, as we have His spirit dwelling within us ungrieved (Eph. iv. 30).

In preparing us to learn this highest of all lessons, the spiritual knowledge of His own internal life, He begins with us by setting before us His outward life, His walk, His words, His sufferings,

His death, etc. From the knowledge of these we learn such lessons as, in our childish condition, we are capable of learning; but the aim of our most gracious Teacher always is to lead us through the outward on to the inward, to lift us higher, and draw us into closer communion with Himself. We see how He was grieved by the slowness of the disciples to follow Him in His leading of them into this loftier sphere. Whatever helps us to know CHRIST better is a benefit to us; but nothing can truly help us, unless it be used for this purpose by the HOLY GHOST.

Excited feelings, and clear, vivid conceptions may be got at meeting and by study, but if these be all, they are utterly worthless, though they are very pleasant. Nothing really profits us which does not empty us more completely of the love of SELF, and of the WORLD; which does not cast us more entirely upon CHRIST ALONE, as EVERYTHING to us; and which does not help us to a more exact conformity to His blessed image. Here lies our great lesson—TO KNOW CHRIST, and in learning it He is our only TEACHER.

And what happiness comes near the happiness of the soul that is being thus taught of *God?* With *God* ever communicating Himself in fuller measures and in new ways; and with the child of GOD ever opening his heart to take in those most blessed communications, gladly making ready room for their reception by casting out of it self and the world more thoroughly, the communion of the saint thus carried on is even now very glorious. His responsive faith welcomes unceasingly the rich gifts of Divine grace, while Divine grace delights to pour out its treasures into the bosom of such a receptive faith.

3. THE LOVE OF THE TRUTH.

ONE of the great wants of the day is not so much the KNOWLEDGE OF THE TRUTH, as the " LOVE OF THE TRUTH " (2 Thess. ii. 10), without which the truth itself can bring no blessing. For this needful (indispensable) LOVE OF TRUTH, we ought to seek on our faces from God, who alone is able to work it in us.

Divine truth, like the sun, shines with its own bright light ; but just as the light of the sun needs an eye to discern it, for the blind cannot see it, so Divine truth is not rightly seen except by those who have susceptible souls.   Others, looking on God's truth, pervert it into a lie (Matt. vi. 22, 23).

It was so with the Pharisees of old. They studied Scripture as no class of modern religionists do; and yet, having the wrong state of soul to begin with, they conceived in their own minds a portraiture of the promised Messiah DIAMETRICALLY OPPOSITE to what the actual Christ was to be. And so when the true Christ came, they pronounced Him to be not incarnate God, but an incarnate devil (John viii. 48, 49), and crucified the real Christ in the interests of their ideal Christ. Because it was the truth which Jesus spoke to them, they rejected both it and Him (John viii. 45). Because it was true, it seemed incredible to them; loving lies, and feeding on ashes, they could do nothing else with the truth which condemned them (Isa. xliv. 20).

This is the way the fleshly mind generally acts with God's truth, even when to appearance it accepts it (see Rom. viii. 7, 8). The natural man dislikes the truth of God, whether in law or in Gospel.

Is it not also to be feared that the truth of God is sometimes handled, not merely by natural men, but also by those who, while renewed by grace, are in a backsliding state, and have great remainders of corruption about them, which bias them in such a way that it becomes sadly perverted?

It behoves us then to return individually to the pure fountain-head, even to the Word of God itself, if we would be kept from error; and it is still more necessary that, in studying the Word of God, we be under the special teaching of the Holy Spirit ; for, apart from Him, our own fleshly minds shall certainly mislead us.

The abounding errors which are abroad, because of this total lack of all harmony between the light in which God puts things before us, and the light in which fleshly man looks at them, are so many, that to attempt detail is impossible. Shall I advert to one merely, and that a very common one ? It refers to what is understood generally by the word SALVATION. What really does salvation mean ? Now, I am bold to say that when God speaks of salvation He means more than many do when they read, or hear, or speak, or preach of it. For fallen man can look on the salvation of which he is told in no other than an entirely selfish spirit ; and in looking at it in this spirit, he can only have a limited view of what God means by salvation.

To be brief, then, let me simply say that SIN is an evil so immense that there is no real evil in the universe but itself ; and its evil lies in its *essential*

nature, not in its mere accompaniments.   All its
results are evil ; but even though this had not
been the case, sin would have been in itself no
less horrible and hateful.   Now, while the holy
God hates the sin itself, man loves the sin itself,
and hates its painful consequences.   Remove these,
and you make sin delicious to him (Job xv. 16).
In this spirit, then, hearing that God has provided
salvation at such cost out of His mere love to
sinners, he thinks of this salvation as being a
deliverance from the thing about the sin that
caused him pain and uneasiness—namely, its everlasting penalty.   But God, in providing salvation,
has been thinking of, and aiming at, deliverance, not
merely from the penalty, but also from the SIN
ITSELF (Matt. i. 21 ; Gal. i. 4).   Hence, when God
in His Word offers to every man free salvation, and
when man reads this offer of salvation, God's
thoughts and man's thoughts about the thing
which is being actually offered are frequently quite
different, and so a fatal mistake is often made.

The salvation which God speaks of, and presses
upon the sinner, includes in it an entire forsaking
of the sin itself, and of all that the flesh cares
to have (Luke xiv. 33).   The hating even of one's
own fallen self-life (Luke xiv. 26), the crucifixion

of the flesh (Gal. v. 24), and this daily (Luke ix. 23) and carried out to a very trying extent (1 Cor. ix. 27) ; and the total surrender of all that one has, and is, into the hands of Christ.

This is what I understand to be the meaning of the word SALVATION.

I think, therefore, that the great point to be aimed at is, that we look at the TRUTH; and this equally whether it be dark or bright—it is the truth that saves us; it is through the belief of pleasant lies that men destroy themselves. And all along, the greatest difficulty in dealing with sinners is just this, they cannot be persuaded to look at the whole truth, especially the dark side of things.

Now the blessed Gospel sets before us things that are the very blackest of the black, and also things that are the brightest of the bright ; and we must faithfully receive both, and submit our hearts to the mighty influence of both—on no account may we pick and choose, to please ourselves, among the holy words of GOD; EVERY word of GOD is pure ; and we need the terrible quite as much as we need the consolatory. It is the terrible that is oftenest needed, and that is also far the most likely to be neglected.

CHAPTER XXV.

GOD IS ALL-SUFFICIENT.

1. Have Faith in God.

THE subject is one of great importance, and also a fruitful one. The Lord Himself is our grand example in this, as in all besides; but the Bible furnishes us with very many minor examples, useful to us to study, and to receive encouragement from. David at Ziklag (1 Sam. xxx. 6) occurs to me. He had been annointed long before to be king over Israel, and like all the Lord's servants who have been called to special service, he found that such call involves in the first place sorrow and suffering. At length, in a season of depressed faith, his sorrows seemed to be unbearable, and he went out of *the land of Israel* altogether, to dwell among the Philistines. He had done so once before, and had found his new circumstances in Gath so distressing that he had been led to feign

madness; but, as the present is always the worst
(as we think), he had forgotten his old experiences
in Gath, and goes back to it. Poor David!
Achish gives him Ziklag for a residence, and here
he behaves in a very sad way indeed. An Israelite
had better stay where God sets him in the land of
Israel; our own shifts only make matters worse.

At last war breaks out between the Philistines
and Israel. What shall David do now? He can
rightly take no side; and yet he must. God
delivered him out of his sore perplexity into which
his own self-willed shifts had brought him; and so
the Philistine chiefs refuse to retain him in the
Philistine army. Moody and downcast he returns
with his rejected warriors home. Home! he has
none now. There are the smoking ruins of it;
and his wives and children are—he knows not
where. And now his angry comrades, laying all
the blame on him, purpose to stone him. Could
desolation be more complete? What does he do?
What can he do? He *encourages himself* IN THE
LORD HIS GOD. He sought his support in uttermost desolation in the Lord, and in the Lord as
being his God. And see the issue. The battle
which was then about to take place killed Saul and
Jonathan, and cleared David's way at once to the

throne; and as for the wives and children carried off, he recovered them ere they were well made captives. Had David foreseen how he should have been placed within forty-eight short hours, he could not have shed a tear, he would have sung for very gladness. Instead of this being a fresh sorrow —heavier than all that before had come upon him— it was the time of his emancipation from all his great sorrows. God, who foresaw it all (who in truth was working it all out), was not a bit troubled for David's sake; and David, if he had trusted God more simply, would not have been troubled either.

This is faith—to leave all our concernments to the disposal of Divine, Almighty love and wisdom.

We have the same warrant to do so that David had—and more. We shall find the same comfort and strength in it that David did; and the same issue of all shall be very blessed, in our case as in David's. We know not whither we are being led, but God knows His own selected road for us, and we follow His trusted leading with quiet, happy blindness.

How many souls this day are very sorely burdened with the pressure of cares and sorrows that are felt to be almost too much for them! At the same time, how many are there again, placed in circumstances *just as sorrowful*, just as alarming, who are almost, or altogether, free from any burden or sorrowful pressure! They have got a release from this painful pressure by means of the sheer carelessness and unconcern which is one of the most debased conditions of soul possible to fallen man. But how very small is the number who, being placed in circumstances of trial like the first class referred to, are as free from all care and trouble about it as the second class is; while they owe this exemption from care, not to their stupid carelessness, but solely to their FAITH IN GOD. They cast all their burden on heavenly love, and walk forth with free and unencumbered heart, caring for nothing but one thing—that they may perfectly serve the holy will of God.

PERFECT peace is to be reached only through PERFECT faith and PERFECT patience—the faith and the patience which stand prepared for whatsoever it may please God to permit and to appoint. I am greatly struck by the degree of holy confidence in Psalm xlvi. 1, 2, 3, and if Jewish faith could soar so high, how calm and abiding should our rest of heart be!

2. GOD'S HEDGE.

A little verse has been making music in my
heart for several days past. Shall I venture to suggest
it to you? It is Job i. 10. Though the words
were spoken by the father of lies, they are
perfectly true; though uttered in malignity, they
are filled with sweetest consolation. " THOU hast set
an hedge about HIM, and about *his house*, and
about ALL THAT HE HAS, on EVERY side." What a
picture of a man in absolute security! God keeps
him—and He equally keeps HIS—nay, ALL that is
his; and He keeps from every danger. We have
this blessing already in Christ. May He give us
the very fullest measure of confiding faith in the
Divine assurance, so that like David under sore
trial, we shall even say, "I will both lay me down
in peace and *sleep;* for Thou, Lord, only makest
me dwell in safety" (Ps. iv. 8).

3. GOD'S PRESENCE.

GOD says, " MY PRESENCE shall go with thee,"
and I will give thee rest (Exod. xxxiii. 14). And
it shall be very strange indeed if that presence,
which we expect shall be able by itself to fill up

eternity for us with rapture, shall not be able to make more than tolerable the little fragment of life here, which now remains for us. For myself, I desire heartily to pass through my small remainder of pilgrimage " LEANING " as I have never leant " on the Beloved," and if, in order to bring this about, it be indispensable that earth be turned into a tenfold wilderness to me than it has ever been—then " AMEN," let Christ be everything to me.

---

4. GOD'S GRACE.

WHAT a blessed assurance was that given to Paul in 2 Cor. xii. 9 ; and given equally to you and to me ! Our burden may be heavy, and our need may be urgent, but His grace shall be always sufficient ; and He shall not suffer the trial at any time to go beyond the strength supplied (1 Cor. x. 13). But it is HIS grace, not OURS ; we always feel the weakness, while He supplies the strength that meets the need. Let us then walk in joyous trust and humble dependence, comforted by knowing that though we be poor and needy, the Lord is planning for us (Ps. xl. 17).

2:15

5. A CLOSE WALK WITH GOD.

I AM constantly pressing on myself (and which I pray God to give me) the maintenance of a close and constant walk with God. *Always*, and *everywhere*, and in *everything* let our communion with Him be kept up unbroken. Doctrines, however clearly seen, or firmly held, will never, never meet the urgent wants of the soul. It is God we need —God Himself. God in Christ. And we may always enjoy His presence. He is constantly speaking to us ; but alas, few, few have ears to hear Him (see the word "IF" in Rev. xiii. 9). He speaks to us in His word ; let us listen to Him speaking there. He speaks in His daily providence, He speaks to us in our hearts, but He speaks in such a very still small voice, that unless we carefully listen to Him we shall miss it, for the din and clamour of a noisy world, and of our own trifling hearts, will quite drown His voice. Oh, what lives of heaven begun on earth might we lead if we were only believing and faithful !

CHAPTER XXVI.

THANKSGIVING.

1. In everything give Thanks.

THERE is no exercise which is more becoming to creatures like ourselves than hearty thanksgivings to God. Deserving *only* His wrath, and receiving ONLY the very fulness of His tender mercy, how fervent should our thanksgivings be! "Bless the Lord, O my soul, and all that is within me bless His holy name" (Ps. ciii. 1). And yet it is to be feared that there is very little of it, that there is humbling reason to complain both of ourselves and of our fellows. "Oh that MEN would praise the Lord for His goodness, and for His wonderful works to the children of men!" (Ps. cvii. 15).

Suffering will set even a prayerless man to praying; but if deliverance come to him, he omits the giving of thanks for it,

> For lips cry, " God be merciful,"
> That ne'er cried, " God be praised."

Ten lepers besought mercy at Christ's hands, but
only one of the ten returned to give God glory for
the miracle vouchsafed (Luke xvii. 13–18). And
so it is still.

The believer ought to be free from this ungrate-
ful spirit. And as a matter of fact he will be free
from it just in so far as he is delivered from selfishness. No exercise can be more delightful to an
humble, unselfish, and loving heart, than to recount
God's goodness, in His own presence, and offer to
Him the solemn sacrifices of thanksgiving on
account of it. Let me add that no ministry is
more acceptable to God or more glorifying (Ps.
l. 23).

We should thank God for every mercy we
receive (Ps. cxxxvi. 1–3), and that would occupy us
constantly ; we should give thanks at every remembrance of His awful holiness (Ps. xcvii. 12). In
the assured faith that all things are working
together for our good, whether we see that it is so
or not (Rom. viii. 28), we should give thanks for
everything, as Job did in his sore trial (Job i. 21) ;
as Jesus did when His countrymen were rejecting
Him (Matt. xi. 25). Dear old Chrysostom was

constantly saying, " Thanks be to God for every-thing ; " he died with the words in his lips.

Yes, we should give thanks to God in all circumstances, and for all He is doing (Eph. v. 20 ; 2 Cor. ix. 11). Whatever He does is the perfection of wisdom and of love, and *faith*, believing that it is so, can thank Him for it, though the trusting man cannot see how it is to work out good to any one. Especially should every prayer abound in thanksgiving. It is greatly wanting if it does not (Phil. iv. 6). And while we thank God for mercies to ourselves, we lovingly thank Him also for His goodness to others, and this not only in regard to His goodness to our friends, but to the whole Church (1 Thess. i. 2)—nay, to the whole world (1 Tim. ii. 1).

---

2. God's Infinite Goodness.

How good is our God and Father ! If one would endeavour to speak of His wonderful works which He has done, and His gracious words which He has spoken, and His deep thoughts of loving kindness which He cherishes *to usward*, one is overpowered, for when we would declare and speak of them, they are more than can be numbered (Ps.

xl. 5). His goodness, in itself, is INFINITE; nay, more than this, you and I can each say, tremulous with joyous wonder, His goodness TO ME has been *infinite*——and I know as yet only a very little about the beginning of it. Oh, what abandonment of love, what devotedness of obedience, what fervour of gratitude, what unlimited trust, becomes creatures so unworthy, and yet so wonderfully dealt with!

There are, therefore, always abundant matters for hearty thanksgiving; all that is needed is a ready mind. But it is only the humble who are really fitted to enjoy this delightful ministry of thanksgiving.

------

3. DIVINE KEEPING.

THE mightiest, kindest, and softest of hands are busied about us both night and day. Let us lay ourselves down in the assured faith of this, and rest on it as on a pillow of down; for it is not *our care* in keeping ourselves, but *His care* in keeping us that really can preserve us from evil. We always *need* gracious Divine keeping: thank God we always have it.

------

4. MERCY ON THE BACK OF MERCY.

WHAT wondrous mercy have we seen—loads of it—positive back burdens of it (Ps. lxviii. 19); mercy on the back of mercy, nothing else in fact but mercy. And now, in the spirit of self-emptied pilgrims, we desire to wait patiently for the final mercy here—the permission to lay aside this body of sin and death. And we expect eternity to be filled with the marvellous display of mercies of the most astounding magnitude (Eph. ii. 7). Oh, to be enabled to spend the few remaining days of our life here in true humility—the uttermost humility —and the loving devotedness of obedience and thanksgiving !

5. LOVE WHICH PASSETH KNOWLEDGE.

THE astonishing fact that dust and ashes like us —sinful dust and ashes—are IN CHRIST made, what no other creature ever has been, the sons and daughters of the Lord Almighty—this is a love which passeth knowledge, the length, and breadth, and depth, and height of which are unutterable, and ought to fill our hearts with the deepest praise and thanksgiving. May we *pray*, and *think*, and *act*, and *suffer*, and *die* under the joyous, sanctifying influence of the assured faith of it.

---

6. WHOSE I AM.

WHAT a most cheering thought, that we belong to the Lord Jesus—are His *very own* (John xiii. 1)! Did we realise the fact that we are given to Him to be His own by the Father (John xvii. 24), chosen by Himself (John xv. 16), purchased at the cost of His life (1 Cor. vi. 19), rescued by His power (Luke xi. 22 ; Gal. i. 4), and surrendered to Him to be our only Lord and Portion, it would not only fill our hearts with the deepest gratitude and thanksgiving, but it would also increase our desire to be enabled to live daily as CHRIST'S OWN (Ps. xlv. 10, 11).

---

7. SHALL I COMPLAIN ?

COMPLAIN ! anything rather than that. God has dealt with me all my life long in a love which is INFINITE, and with a wisdom that is incapable of making any mistakes. I feel it then a privilege, quite as much as a duty, to lay myself at His feet, and beg of Him of His grace to arrange all the circumstances of my lot just as HE HIMSELF SEES BEST, and to thank Him most gratefully for them all.

---

8. Some Special Mercies.

THERE are some who, if they were to make up a list of their chiefest earthly mercies, would make it run in some such style as this. While deeply grateful for all earthly comforts, they are still more thankful for the withdrawal of them. They will say : " God charged me solemnly to lay aside every weight, warning me of the consequences if I did not obey. But I did not quite believe what He said, and so I did not obey ; and now, in very love to me, He has Himself stripped off the most dangerous of my weights, and has set me free. He warned me that my cherished right eye, and my prized right hand and foot, were likely to work me woe, and He bade me pluck out the eye, and cut off hand and foot; for He said it was better to grope my way with one eye into heaven, or halt or maimed to enter the eternal glory, than to march with healthy eyes and feet, into the bottomless pit. But I could not find courage to do it, for I did not

believe that my danger was so very urgent; and
so in very pity to me, He plucked out my eye, and
cut off hand and foot; and now, with Him to lead
me, nay, to carry me in His bosom, as a shepherd
carries some helpless lamb, I am happier far than
when I had eyes and hands and feet. Yes, these
are some of the special mercies in which the lively
saint finds his ground for chiefest gratitude, praise,
and thanksgiving.

---

9. A RETROSPECT.

I AM filled with wonder, love, and praise, when
I look back on my life; it is so different from what
I had planned for myself. Like all thinking
youths, I had my own plans about myself, but God
had also His plans; and His plans were infinitely
BETTER than mine. Indeed, there has been in
it everything that I would have shunned. I do
believe that if, fifty years ago, the Lord had laid
before me what my life was to be, I would have
shrunk with horror from the vision, and would
have cried to Him to let me die at once rather
than face it all. And yet, now, when it is over, I
look back on it with a thankfulness I cannot
express. He has arranged it all in wonderful love

and wisdom. Indeed, I know nobody anywhere with whom I would consent to change lots. With all my heart I say, in view of my life, " As for God, HIS way is PERFECT " (Ps. xviii. 30). No doubt He, in infinite love, put me into the furnace, but He also stepped in beside me ; and with Him carrying me in His bosom I found it sweet to be there. It was easy for me to glorify Him when IN THE FIRES (Isa. xxiv. 15). He fulfilled to me (and more than fulfilled) His word in Isa. xliii. 2 ; Hab. iii. 19. Yes, it has been the CREAM of my life.

------

10. DIVINE APPOINTMENT.

THE man who rests in the will of God in simple faith and love is always happy, perfectly contented, and full of praise and thanksgiving. His lot may be very trying, but he trusts the love and the wisdom of Him who has appointed it all, he meekly accepts the Divine appointment ; he sees that the meek endurance of his troubles is the very service which his Lord and Owner has set him to discharge, and he rejoices with a joy unspeakable at the thousands of opportunities which the sorrows of his lot afford him for delightful communion with his God and Father. He sees that his lot is perfectly fitted for him, and he is fitted for his lot; and thus walking with God, he is happy, "blessing the Lord at all times," and "His praise continually in his mouth" (Ps. xxxiv. 1).

---

11. "They that sow in Tears shall reap in Joy."

Our circumstances may be very sorrowful when nature, in its unbelief, looks on them; but the sorrow loses every trace of bitterness when faith takes them out of a loving Father's hand. Faith looks on them as seeds, seeds which God Himself has sown, and sown with the design of producing from them a glorious and everlasting harvest. And when faith looks on the matter in that light, then hope springs up, and, in her eagerness, anticipates the glorious crop which shall surely come—and even now she begins to exult in the harvest-joy. And now our estimate of the affliction becomes completely changed. The poverty, the sickness, the trial of whatever kind, is recognised as the indispensable condition under which it is meant that we should ENJOY GOD; without it we should never have sought God so eagerly as we have been constrained to do, nor should we have so found Him, nor should we have been able to take in so much of His fulness. Instead, then, of feeling dejected by our present trials, let our faith even now forecast the glorious harvest into which they are meant to ripen, and let us think of that day of wonders when "THEY THAT SOW IN TEARS SHALL REAP IN JOY" (Ps. cxxvi. 5; 2 Cor. iv. 17). "Wherefore comfort one another with these words."

---

12. A THOUSAND SMALL GIFTS.

How sweet are all the mercies of God to the soul that delights in them—not for their own sake, not for the enjoyment they can be made to furnish to the earthly self-life, but that delights in them as manifestations of the most wonderful love to us of our Heavenly Father. The thousand small gifts of His daily providence, received in this spirit, become precious and sanctifying to us, and they each call for the deepest thanksgiving.

13. A REMEDY FOR A HEAVY HEART.

WHEN you are cast down and in heaviness, do you ever kneel down and address God through Christ in hearty thanksgivings? I mean thanksgivings, and nothing else—no petition, no adoration, no confession even—only thanking Him for His mercies. Often, often, over and over again, have I got rid of sore fits of gloom and dejection by means of this. If I was spiritually dejected, and could take only low ground before God (and this was generally the case), I took low ground; only it is all important that one be honest and without guile in dealing with God — pretending to be nothing but just what we are, to feel nothing but just what we feel. And whatever our actual condition may be, there is always plenty in it for which to thank God. One can at least say (as I have often had to begin by saying), I thank Thee heartily, O God, that I am OUT OF HELL. I thank Thee that Thou hast borne so long with a grievous sinner like me. I thank Thee that Thou didst send Thy blessed Gospel to me, that Thou didst continue to press it on me, that Thou hast not accepted my refusals of it, nor been indignant at my delays and my treacherous treatment of Thee.

I thank Thee for the pressing offers Thou makest me of ALL the riches of Thy grace, of all the treasures of Thy love—that there is no one more welcome to come to Thee in Christ Jesus as a forgiven, beloved, and accepted child than I, the chief of sinners. And as one goes on, for an hour or more to thank God for mercies—mercies countless as the sands, mercies of childhood, of youth, of riper years — for temporal mercies, for spiritual mercies, for mercies that chastened and mercies that comforted, for mercies so many that "Oh, eternity's required to utter all His praise," because of them; as one goes over this endless list, thanking, thanking, thanking, the gloomy cloud gets thinner and thinner, till it disappears altogether, and the heart, recovering all its former gladness, and even more, cries out: "Why art thou cast down, O my soul, and why art thou disquieted within me? Hope thou in God, for I shall yet praise Him for the help of His countenance" (Ps. xlii. 5). Have you ever tried this? It is my infallible remedy for getting rid of a heavy heart.

CHAPTER XXVII.

JOY.

1. THE LACK OF JOY.

THE lack of joy, I think, is often owing to one or other of two causes. First, The man does not clearly apprehend the PERFECT FREENESS of saving grace; that, if he be saved at all, the grace which does it MUST BE FREE. He does not see and feel himself to be a mere SINNER, and nothing else; while the Lord Jesus receiveth none except those who come to Him as mere sinners, and as nothing else. And so the anxious soul is kept from peace often for years, because it waits till it shall have made itself a little better before it thinks it shall be fit for the Saviour. All this is a terrible mistake; but so soon as the man *actually comes* to the Lord, confessing that he is a mere SINNER, and nothing else whatever, then at once the gracious Saviour floods his wondering soul with peace and joy.

240

But when the young disciple loses this first joy, as often is the case, he generally falls back into his old mistake ; and he may keep himself in his misery for long, simply because he does not see that the Lord JESUS deals with us from first to last in the way of perfect grace, and that the erring believer must deal with his SAVIOUR *till the very end*, as one who, *even yet* is in himself a mere sinner, and nothing else. Now, while the back-slidden disciple is reluctant to keep on this low ground, which is the only ground on which the Lord will meet him, peace continues more or less to be a stranger to his bosom.

And besides this, there is a SECOND very common cause of a Christian's joylessness. He often walks carelessly. He does not watch and pray, that he enter not into temptation. He grieves the HOLY SPIRIT, and in this case, for the erring man's own good, the grieved Spirit will certainly withdraw His abused consolations.

Oh, how delightful it is to think of the unutterable love and grace of the blessed Lord ! He will welcome any sinner, however vile ; He will forgive any sin, however atrocious ; and He will tenderly lay the beloved forgiven one in His bosom. But, oh, how solemn it is to think on His equally

2:16

unutterable holiness! He loathes SIN; and He will not continue to lavish the tokens of His love on any forgiven one who still tampers with the forbidden and loathed thing. Christ can have no concord with Belial; and we must come sheer out from all our past evil, and must no longer TOUCH the unclean if we expect God to receive us, and to be a FATHER to us (2 Cor. vi. 15–18).

Now, I verily believe that most of the joylessness of Christians come from their overlooking either the *infinite grace,* or the *infinite* holiness of GOD.

---

2. JOY IN GOD.

OUR lack of joy often arises from our want of realising the Divine presence, and its accompanying blessedness. I believe that we shall individually enjoy these just in proportion as we yield ourselves up to *Him.* For God is always present here and now, and this as truly as He is in heaven; only there are none save the spiritually susceptible who discern and enjoy the glorious glorifying vision. To see Him by faith is to be made HOLY (2 Cor. iii. 18); to see Him by sight shall be to be

GLORIFIED (1 John iii. 2). And it is the Divine life in us which alone can enable us to discern, and to rejoice in the fulness of eternal life, which is in God as its fountain ; and to the fellowship of which in Christ Jesus we have been most graciously called. Instead, then, of postponing our enjoyment of God's presence till death, let us eagerly open out our hearts to receive as much as we can hold of it even now, and to turn our earthly lives into heavenly by making them a continual walking with God in the light (1 John i. 7).

We may have as much of God's presence here and now as we are capable of enjoying : and His presence would not only sweeten all, but fill our hearts with holy joy. Infinitely better ANY WORST with Him, than ANY BEST without Him. Nay, so prone are we to slip aside from Him, that it is as gain to be so circumstanced, that one NEEDS HIM CONSTANTLY, and cannot get on at all without His realised presence.

" I would commune with Thee, my God, e'en to Thy seat
    I come ;
  I leave my joys, I leave my sins, and seek in Thee my
      home.
  Oh, this is life ! oh, this is joy ! my God to find Thee so ;
  Thy face to see, Thy voice to hear, and all Thy love to
    know."

How much reason have we continually to sing of the mercy of the Lord ; good is He when He gives, and just as good when He pleases to take away. Worthy, ever worthy of our heartfelt joyous praises. Our calling as the followers of the " Man of Sorrows " is to outward trial—to constant conflict, and unwearied self-denial. We are utter strangers here, and thankfully let us accept the usage which the world gives to its strangers (John xv. 19). But our calling is to inward joy, joy in God, joy in the Lord, joy of the Holy Ghost's operation, joy unspeakable (1 Peter i. 8) and without end. And we have abundant reason for this joy, though, like Levi, we have no inheritance among our neighbours (Josh. xiv. 3, 4). Yet, like Levi too, we have the Lord Himself for our inheritance (chap. xiii. 33). Not creatures, not God's gifts even, but God Himself in Christ Jesus is our true portion. Then, that is a *blessing* which helps to empty the heart of all earthly creature consolations, and makes it flee for comfort to Him who is " its EXCEEDING joy " (Ps. xliii. 4), saying, " All my springs are in Thee " (Ps. lxxxvii. 7).

His own words, " that your joy may be full " ought to sink deep into our heart. He exhorts us to joy—to FULL joy—He aims at securing it in

every way (John xv. 11 ; xvi. 24 ; xvii. 13 ;
1 John i. 4). Oh, let us open our hearts to the
sanctifying influence, and seek a degree of joy in
Jesus that is UNSPEAKABLE (1 Peter i. 8).

Has He not given ample grounds for it ? In
Christ, are we not God's own, His very *children ?*
We are dear to His heart as is the Lord Jesus, the
Son of His eternal love. He thinks on us by day,
by night, without intermission; and all His thoughts
are only and always thoughts of love (Jer. xxix. 11).
IIis eye is over us continually to watch for our
safety (Isa. xxvii. 3); as constantly as if He had
nothing else to look after. His mighty arms are
folded round us, protecting each of us as if we were
the one and only treasure of His infinitely loving
heart. My soul, believest thou all this ? if not, why
dost thou profess faith when thou dost not exercise
it ? But believe it with a conviction that is stronger
than the evidence of sight (Heb. xi. 1), then thy
joy cannot but be abundant and perpetual ; as well
as being purely and simply joy in Him—in Him as
being what He is in Himself—and as being what
He is to thee.

And if thou dost believe it, the joy-giving faith
should dispel every groundless grief about the trifling sorrows of earth, and every foolish and torment-

ing fear ; and should leave thee mainly the great
grief that thou dost so feebly respond to love like
God's, and to the great fear lest thou shouldest
dishonour Him, or grieve His Holy Spirit (Eph.
iv. 30).

———

3. TRIUMPHANTLY HAPPY—SIX REASONS FOR BEING SO.

OH, how triumphantly happy might we always
be, if we were to live under the felt power of the
following truths which we profess to believe :—

1st, That God is LOVE; pure love, infinite, eternal,
and unchangeable love, and that all that He does
is done in perfect love.

2nd, That God has infinite wisdom; that He
never makes mistakes, cannot do so; that He
always does only what is good, and always does
what is the *one very best thing*.

3rd, That God is Almighty, that He meets no
difficulties in carrying out His purposes of wisdom
and love; and no one can resist His might (Job
xlii. 1, 2).

4th, That His Providence is but His Almighty
power acting under the direction of His unerring
wisdom and His infinite love ; and that this provid-

ence of His is arranging and disposing of every circumstance of our lot—every one—down to the number of our hairs (Matt. x. 30). Not a sparrow falls without Him.

5th, That this wonderful Being is, in Christ Jesus, MY OWN FATHER, and has made me His dearly beloved child ; that He has forgiven me all my sins, fully, freely, and for ever ; that all His immensity of love, and wisdom, and power, are being exercised about me and all my concerns *every moment ;* and that He has put away everything that once *separated* Him from me as completely as if there had never been any separation.

And *6th*, That this great God, my Father who thus cares for me, and has engaged to provide for me, has strictly forbidden me to be anxiously careful about myself (1 Peter v. 7 ; Phil. iv. 6 ; Matt. vi. 25). He bids me, if I love Him, to show my love, by trusting Him that He will do everything which He promises to do. Oh, how we might honour God, and enjoy His faithful love however we may be circumstanced, if we only *believed,* BELIEVED, truly BELIEVED these plain and undeniable truths.

4. FULL OF GLADNESS.

Let this loving and holy Redeemer be everything
to us, and we need nothing more to fill us as full of
gladness as we can hold. I believe that the full
clear vision of Christ's glory for only five minutes,
and along with that, the sweet, the most sweet
enjoyment of His love, would be an ample and
satisfying reward to any soul for a long life of
service and of suffering, even unto death. But God
means us not for a mere five minutes of this
seraphic joy, but for a whole endless eternity of it,
for which he is preparing us. Nay, more; He
means us to enter on the enjoyment of it, as we are
able here and now. And I do believe that we may,
in the present time, enjoy the blessedness of heaven
far, FAR more than most of us do, than most of us
think. Let us covet earnestly this gift of God
—this dwelling of Christ in our hearts by His
Holy Spirit—bringing with Him joy and gladness ;
yea, a very heaven into our souls.

---

5. GOD'S GIFT TO US AND GOD'S GIFT TO CHRIST.

THE lively Believer rejoices in God's matchless
gift to him of his Beloved Son ; and, at favoured

moments, his heart swells, almost to bursting, with a joy that is unspeakable and full of glory. Now, it will not diminish his joy, but will increase it, if he thinks that, while he is rejoicing in Christ as the peerless gift of God to himself, Christ also is rejoicing in *him*, as being the Father's gift of love to Him. O Believer, is it not most wonderful and delightful to know that thou, even THOU, art a welcome and beloved love-gift from the Father to the Son of God, even as that Son is a precious gift to thee. Such is His matchless love, that He rejoices over us incomparably more than we, with our narrow hearts, are able to rejoice over Him. And so in Luke xv. 5-7, when depicting the finding of the lost sinner by the seeking Saviour, it is not the sinner's joy in being saved that is referred to, it is the far greater joy of the Saviour in finding His wandered lost one. No doubt the sinner rejoices ; but his joy is nothing compared with Christ's.

---

6. A Joyous Life.

WHAT a joyous thing a life becomes, whatever may be its outward circumstances, when it is spent with God and in Christ ; when the man feels that he has nothing to think of but God and His Christ; no one to speak with in his solitude but that God who never fails to pour the secrets of His love into any ear that is joyously opened to receive them; and who has no business to concern himself with except how best he may please and enjoy GOD. Nothing can dim the brightness or spoil the sweetness of such a life, "Hid with Christ in GOD." Nay, I almost venture to say that so bright, so sweet, does the Divine presence, by itself, make such a life, that nothing added to this presence can make the life either brighter or sweeter. He who so lives lacks nothing good. And anyone may live it if he choose. May this life be yours, and mine, and that in the fullest measures possible to man on earth, and since God is willing, WHY SHOULD IT NOT BE SO ?

CHAPTER XXVIII.

PERSEVERANCE OF THE SAINTS.

THE great truth of perseverance is most clearly taught in the Holy Scriptures. When the Lord begins a good work He will surely finish it (Phil. i. 6). HIS election secures from POSSIBILITY of fatal deception (Matt. xxiv. 24). None CAN pluck out of His hand (John x. 29). Whom His love sets apart for Himself, His Omnipotence preserves (1 Peter i. 5). But this truth, like all other truths, has its companion truth; from which if we separate it, it operates virtually as an error. God's Omnipotence shall keep the saint; but this keeping shall be carried out through the saint's continued believing (1 Peter i. 5). Perseverance then becomes a human duty as well as a Divine gift. It has a place in the Christian *Code* quite as distinctly as in the *Creed*. Nay, I do think that it would be less dangerous to drop it out of one's Creed (great loss though this would be), than to drop it out of the Code. And I am encouraged to say so from the fact that, while I have met with but few Christians who suffered very seriously from defective views of perseverance, I meet often with souls who suffer serious damage from a most unjustifiable abuse of it. When a man's spiritual health is such that he has little or no comfort except what he finds in the doctrine of perseverance, the sooner he drops that comfort the better and the safer for himself, and turns to seek it instead in CLOSER *fellowship* with Christ.

I am struck with the fact that neither our Lord nor His apostles are in the least degree afraid of compromising this blessed doctrine of perseverance. He warns disciples that whatever branches IN HIM are unfruitful, they shall be *cut off* and BURNED (John xv. 2–6). He speaks of some who " for a while BELIEVE and who yet fall away (Luke viii. 13). He warns Jews who BELIEVE that there is a very solemn " IF " in the matter (John viii. 31, 32). A similar warning, with a similar " IF " in it, Paul repeats in Heb. iii. 14, addressed to " holy brethren " (ver. 1). Peter carries the warning quite as far in 2 Peter i. And here too with an " IF " (ver. 8). He addresses saints who believe (ver. 1), were *regenerated* (ver. 4), but who are urged to exercise *utmost* DILIGENCE *to* ADD TO FAITH other graces (vers. 5–7), with the warning that IF they did so the issue would be blessed (ver. 8) ; but IF NOT, far otherwise.   Nay, Paul can speak such startling words as we find in Heb. vi. 4–6.

The one set of passages is true, so too is the other.   Let us not cancel the one by the other ; nor yet *subtract* the one from the other, trying to live by the poor *remainder ;* but let us ADD the one to the other, and submit our hearts and souls to the mighty impulses of the grand *sum total.*

CHAPTER XXIX.

THE DEVIL'S SIEVE.

THE Devil's Sieve is a very sorrowful experience. Oh, how many tears have God's children shed in it—precious tears, that are all put carefully past in God's bottle (Ps. lvi. 8) ! But though it be very distressing ofttimes to be tossed mercilessly about in Satan's cruel sieve, and tossed, too, with the most malicious design against us, it is well to remember that he is doing what he does only by special permission (Luke xxii. 31), and within carefully measured limits; that nicest tenderest love is carefully (how carefully !) superintending the whole—love that will not suffer one hair of our heads to perish. We are in the hands of One who loved us better than His own life, and who, in permitting Satan to sift us, is merely using the enemy as HIS MINISTER to us for GOOD.

For we need this thorough winnowing ! how

otherwise could we come to know ourselves, and how, without knowing ourselves, could we come to know Him? And how, without the discovery of it, could the chaff be separated from us *with* OUR OWN FULL CONSENT? Alas! what heaps of worthless chaff fill our hearts—in fact, at first, there is little more than mere chaff in us at all, though we suspect it not. And all that chaff *must* be winnowed out and burned, since nothing but the pure wheat of God's grace in us can be taken with us into the heavenly garner—hence the trying process of the winnowing, trying, indeed, but most lovingly, and most patiently, and most wisely conducted. Those whom God loves best, get the biggest share of it (Heb. xii. 6–12). Let us, then, courageously surrender ourselves into *our heavenly* FATHER'S trusted hands, desiring nothing, beseeching nothing, but that He fulfil in us ALL the good pleasure of His goodness, and the work of faith with power (2 Thess. i. 11).

In spiritual maladies the worst cases are those in which there is no pain and no distress. I am glad, however, that you have had the courage to be so candid, and I beg that you will permit me, in anything further I may say, to be also perfectly candid with you. Out of what bottomless *depths*,

dear friend, have we to cry to God for help
(Ps. cxxx. 1); but, blessed be His name, there are
no depths so deep that the soul plunged in them is
beyond the range of Divine *pity*, or the reach of
the Almighty arm. He is very gracious when He
hears the voice of the believing cry, and He lifts the
crying one out of the fearful pit and the miry clay,
and sets the trembling feet upon a stable rock
(Ps. xl. 1). Your depths and mine may be
vastly different in respect to their details of
horrors (they are so), but all who are truly saved,
are made to feel that God's infinite mercy has
delivered their souls from THE LOWEST HELL
(Ps. lxxxvi. 13).

It seems to me (but I feel the need of speaking
with caution) that Satan has a hand in our distressing experiences; and God also has His hand in
them; and we, too, have our hand. Satan has a
hand. He first tempts us. When he succeeds in
any measure with us, then he improves his advan-
tage to the intensest aggravation possible of our
spiritual sorrow, and aims at getting us drawn away
from the gentle, humbling, holy sorrows of true
penitence, and at overwhelming us beneath the
violent, unhumbled, unsanctifying horrors of an
outraged conscience, in which horrors unbelief

rather than faith is at work. He *was*, and *is*, and *shall be*, NOTHING but liar and murderer to the end.

And we have our hand. Too often when the temptation comes, we do not, I fear, meet it promptly enough by the "shield of FAITH" (Eph. vi. 12–18). In other words, we do not resort *at once*, as helpless things, to hide ourselves under the feathers of the Almighty wing. Instead of fleeing to Him to hide ourselves, we meet the enemy in our own strength, and meet him to be overcome by him, as a matter of course. And then, when the inevitable sorrow comes, we write bitter things against ourselves—we are *humiliated* rather than *humbled*. The discoveries which have been made to us of ourselves through an experience of the kind, do not lead us to a more adoring, a more joyous estimate of Christ as our Saviour, and to a more hearty, self-forsaking closing with Him as *all* our salvation and *all our desire*. No ; Christ is little more to us after such an experience than He was before it ; and we are unwilling to be made a good deal *less* to *ourselves* than we had been. The issue is rather increased conviction of sinfulness, and a feeling of deeper misery because of *what* WE ARE, than increased *trust in the Lord*

2:17

Jesus and greatly augmented joy IN HIM, as being our sole portion for evermore.

But God also has His blessed and Fatherly hand in our distressing struggle and its sequels ; He who out of our evil can still elicit good. Oh, how frightfully prone we are to trust IN OURSELVES that we are something, and have attained something (Luke xviii. 9) ; and how slow to take, how unsteadfast in keeping, our true place in the dust, ascribing our infinite blessedness to the FREE GRACE of our Heavenly Father. We need again and again to be discovered to ourselves, that we may more fully know what WE ARE, and what HE IS TO US in the Son of His love, and Satan's sore siftings of us are made use of for this end, in a way that is very effectual. Ah, don't you feel that you *need* forgiveness still, FREE *forgiveness*, through the blood of the Lamb ?

In this way too we learn what our fallen nature really is, that *in* THE FLESH, we cannot, *cannot*, CANNOT serve, or please God (Rom. viii. **7**, 8); that, in short, human nature *at its best*, just as at its *worst*, is INCAPABLE of pleasing God. Therefore God permits to us such discoveries of our inherent sinfulness as to bring us literally to our wits' end, not that we may be left in despair, but that our

faith and hope may rest on "JESUS ONLY" (2 Cor.
i. 9, 10). For just as it is with the sinner at first,
none but the convicted care for salvation (that is,
for the Lord Jesus to save them), so is it with the
saint all through ; it is according to the increasing
depth of our conviction that we practically value
and rejoice in "the unsearchable riches of Christ."
Let no depth of conviction, then, ever be permitted
under Satan's misuse of it, to diminish our unwaver-
ing trust in God's grace, through Christ Jesus, or
discourage our resort to Him AS TO OUR FATHER,
in believing prayer (Rom. viii. 32). Let us in our
distress REMEMBER the grace of our blessed Lord.
Let us also MAKE USE OF IT, according to our felt
need. He kills us in order to make us alive ; kills
us to the idolatrous life on self, and on creatures,
that we may be made to live on Himself alone.
He wounds us, but the hand which wounds means
to make us whole.

In applying Christ's salvation to us, the very *first*
operation of the Holy Spirit lies in His convicting
us of sin (John xvi. 9). Till this be done, nothing
else can be done in the way of giving spiritual
blessing. And the Holy Spirit's subsequent
operation shall be more or less decided, just in
proportion as His work of conviction is more or less

deep. And though, in our experience of it, this work of His be very trying, yet it is part of His work on us, AS "THE COMFORTER," for He comforts us *no otherwise* than by revealing Christ in His person, and in His offices to us; a revelation which we are incapable of being comforted by, any further than we are broken in heart. Hence, in addition to His revelation of Christ to us, as meeting all our need, He has first to discover ourselves to us, in order to awaken a sense of need. And this work of discovering ourselves to us, is not limited to the first stage of a Christian's experience. Having begun this work, He goes on with it, laying bare to the soul more and more of its own unutterable loathsomeness, while, at the same time, He opens up more clearly before it, the lengths and breadths, the depths and heights, of Christ's LOVE, and of Christ's fulness of every kind; while He also sweetly disposes the soul to appropriate Christ, and to rest in Him with a joy that is unspeakable (1 Peter i. 8). In this way He comforts us, by increasing our joy, not in ourselves as gracious, but IN THE LORD ALONE.

But through his oversight of the fact that this is the Holy Spirit's method of educating souls, the disciple who is being thus trained is ofttimes sorely distressed. He is overwhelmed by the "DESPERATE

WICKEDNESS " (Jer. xvii. 9, 10) which he discerns
in himself, and fancies that, instead of being merely
a new discovery, it is *a new growth*. In fact, he
is sometimes driven well-nigh to despair. Did he
know, and did he remember, the Holy Spirit's
purpose in so dealing with him, and did he fall in
with it, he would rather *take* courage and comfort
from the deepening conviction of his own *enormous
wickedness* as a fallen creature, and he would seek
all, ALL, ALL his joy in Jesus only, where he
would find it more fully than he could appropriate
it. Let me then remind you, dear Christian friend,
as I have often to remind myself, that God's work
of grace is two-fold. He has to *empty* us as well
as to *fill ;* and He has to empty first, that He may
fill afterwards. How sadly filled have we been—
full of self and of creature loves ; and so, in order
to make room in us for Christ and His Father
(John xiv. 23 ; Eph. iii. 17), the emptying process
must be carried out. And God does it thoroughly.
And we must not mistake the matter, though Satan
may be made use of in this emptying process.
God uses him, but leaves us not to the will of the
cruel one. He lets the enemy loose on us, as on
Job, and seems to leave us in our uttermost weakness in his hands. But while Satan designs one

thing God means another; and He uses Satan's siftings of us like wheat to empty us, as an indispensable pre-requisite to our subsequent filling. It is with the HEART-BROKEN and the "CONTRITE" (*ground to powder*) that the Lord delights to dwell (Ps. xxxiv. 18 ; Isa. lvii. 15 ; Isa. lxvi. 2). And blessed are they whom He thus humbles !

In this way have the Lord's children been led in every age. "I am but dust and ashes," said Abraham. "I am not worthy of the least of all Thy mercies," said Jacob. "I abhor myself," said Job. "I am a worm and no man," said David. "I am as a beast before Thee," said Asaph. "Surely I am more brutish than any man," said Agar. "I am a man of unclean lips,—woe is me !" cried Isaiah. "I am not worthy to loose His shoes," said the Baptist. "I am the CHIEF OF SINNERS," said Paul. And the same Spirit leads the children of God in the same path still (Rom. viii. 14).

"Dearest brother, God alone knoweth how corrupt I am. It is not for nought that I wonder at the mercy of being out of hell." So writes the beloved Charles Simeon, of Cambridge. And again he says, "If you want to know the name of him who will be the most signal monument of grace in heaven, I have no doubt I can tell you."

Says Anthony N. Groves, of Bagdad, " I sometimes feel sadly depressed ; and truly I have reason
to be so, looking back on a worse than useless life."
And this was after a life of singular devotedness.

" I am a sinner, the chief of sinners," writes dear
Mrs. Susan Huntingdon, of America. " I used to
think once that this was extravagant language for
me to adopt; *now*, I feel that it describes the
common estimate which I make of myself."

Thus writes William Carey, the missionary : " I
know the Lord can work by the meanest instruments, but I often question whether it would be for
His honour to work by SUCH A ONE AS ME.
Perhaps it would too much sanction carnal security
and guilty sloth in others, *if a person so deeply
sunk in these evils should meet with an eminent
blessing.*"

" If God's Word did not unequivocally declare
the desperate wickedness of the heart," says Henry
Martyn, " I should sink in despair. Nothing but
infinite grace can save ME. But that which
most grieves me is that I am not *more humbled* at
the contemplation of myself."

Thus writes Howell Harris, the eminent Welsh
evangelist : " Oh, what a rich experience have I
gained from this dangerous tour ! I have had a

more intimate knowledge of the self-love, which, unawares to myself, I had been cherishing in my success. I have seen more of the depth of the wickedness of my nature; and *I marvel that the earth is permitted to support such a monster as I am.*"

"I saw so much of my hellish vileness that I appeared worse to myself than ANY DEVIL," says David Brainerd. And again he says, "For my part, I feel the most vile of any creature living; and, I am sure sometimes, there is not such another existing on this side hell."

"None but God knows what an abyss of corruption is in my heart," says M'Cheyne of Dundee.

"I can truly say of every one I know, I hope he is better than myself," says old Thomas Adams of Wintingham.

"Ye complain of the evils of heart atheism," writes Samuel Rutherford; "but it is to a greater atheist than any man can be, that ye write of that."

"I am a most hypocritical wretch, and not worthy that the earth should bear me," says John Bradford, the martyr.

"Lord, I am hell; and thou art heaven," says his companion martyr, Bishop Hooper.

I might quote similarly to any extent, but weary
you perhaps by quoting so many. I have done so,
simply because my heart goes so fully along with
the beloved mourners, when they thus in dust and
ashes confess their vileness, and cast their crowns
before the feet of the One who is the All
Worthy. Oh, for more of this spirit ; oh, for the
most of this spirit ! I would subscribe to the
words of Brown of Haddington, " I bless God
that I know at least this much about religion—
I am convinced that I am as a beast before
God." And is this not the spirit of the forgiven,
rejoicing, but deeply humbled penitent ? (see Ezek.
xvi. 63).

What then can we expect from this incomparably
deceitful, this desperately wicked (Jer. xvii. 9), this
condemned and denounced self-life, but only sin ?
How can we, after our experience of ourselves, trust
any more in our own hearts ? And surely we are
trusting too much in them, when we are reduced
to deepest distress, and almost to despair, at the
repeated discovery that we are really in ourselves
just as bad as God has been telling us all along we
were. When shall we be taught to count on
NOTHING from our own hearts but further wickedness, and on NOTHING from God but further

goodness; and therefore to find all our confidence and hope in God alone?

I know too well that all this may be abused—as indeed what truth of God's Word cannot? It may be abused by the flesh within ourselves; and it could only be abused by the world, if spoken in their hearing. For, as we need the Spirit of God to enable us to comprehend the revelation of God, we equally need Him for our proper use of that revelation. Therefore, we must see to it that we are handling the things of the Spirit in the power of the Spirit, and in communion with God. And when we are in communion, we cannot misuse the gracious words of God. The Divine seed keeps us from it (1 John iii. 9). For our *spiritual oneness* with Christ, in the new nature, is as REAL a thing, and is as *operative* in our experience, as is our *natural oneness* with Adam, in our old and fallen nature. If we walk—*even one step*—according to the nature which unites to Adam, that step is wrong; if we walk according to the new nature, that is, the Spirit of Christ in us, we go right. And this new NATURE in us hates sin, and hates self because of sin; and watches against sin more than men watch against wild beasts, or savage men.

Our only source of spiritual strength is in

Christ; strength to trust, to love, to serve, to crucify self (Gal. v. 24), to resist the devil (James iv. 7). This daring enemy assailed Christ Himself again and again; but the Lord invariably foiled and vanquished him. He assailed Adam, too, in Eden; and even the innocent Adam fell at the first assault; and the Adam in you and in me, and in all the descendants of Adam, has always fallen before him. But THE CHRIST IN US always stands, and always conquers. And when you or I are overcome by our enemy, it is proof that for the time we have been opposing to Satan not CHRIST but SELF. For Christ is never vanquished; and self is never otherwise.

But in order to enjoy this grace of Christ as the indwelling source of our strength, we need to maintain a constant self-denial; a self-denial that is to extend over the whole sphere of our living. For ALL that we do, down to eating and drinking, we should do—not *for* self, and not *from* self— but for God (1 Cor. x. 31); every thought (2 Cor. x. 5), every word (Col. iv. 6; Matt. xii. 36) is to be devoted to God's glory; nay, our lives now are to be henceforward such that it is no longer we who live them, but *Christ in us* (Gal. ii. 20). And this self-denial the flesh will feel to be dreadfully severe. We are to put our members to death (Col. iii. 5), and rather than allow anything to snare us into sin we are to execute the strong words of Mark ix. 43 to 48. And this spirit is perfectly indispensable (Luke ix. 23, 24; xiv. 26, 33). Every true saint of God has it (1 John iii. 3), and of Christ's genuine disciples *not one*, NOT ONE lives to himself, but all live to the Lord more or less steadfastly (Rom. xiv. 7, 8). And whatever in us does not come out of this new nature is SIN, to be hated, confessed, repented of, and forsaken (Rom. xiv. 23). Most of this, dear friend, seems to be utterly unknown in this day of easy profession and religious self-indulgence. But we must judge ourselves, else we shall be judged by the Lord (1 Cor. xi. 31, 32). Of course we all fail; and no one fails more than (perhaps SO MUCH as) I do. But we must confess our failure (1 John i. 9), and repent of it, and watch and pray against temptation and its repetitions; and draw nearer than ever to our most gracious, loving, and Almighty Lord, more humbled, more dependent, more consecrated than ever. And if we fail ten times in an hour, we must then resort to Him ten times in an hour. Oh, how this discipline humbles, but how it also comforts—comforts however in JESUS ONLY.

It costs us nothing whatever TO GET salvation, the Lord so delights to bestow it. But it costs us everything that the self-life cares for to WORK OUT salvation, for the true salvation effects the total destruction of the self-life in us.

I am so thankful to see that you have consecrated yourself. Do not be discouraged by *any* failure. God is for us; who against us? Count your consecration a *settled* matter, and seek strength to live it out. Yes, settled on His part, as well as on yours. Note the word "*acceptable*" in Rom. xii. 1; and deal about your failure, not with God at Sinai, but at Calvary.

I most heartily commend you in all your need to the Infinitely Loving and Almighty Heavenly Father, whose sufficient grace is perfected only in the weakness of the helpless trusting creature (2 Cor. xii. 9). May He fulfil to you Phil. iv. 19; and also Eph. iii. 20. Don't be discouraged. See from 1 Peter v. 9 that "your brethren" (I mean the genuine disciples), while "in the world," are similarly afflicted. Press on! Our real help lies in communion with God as Christ's very members. And when we wait on Him, He fulfils to us the delightful words of Isa. xl. 28–31; yea, the "worm

Jacob" is enabled to thresh the mountains into chaff (Isa. xli. 14, 15).

I feel my heart very tenderly drawn out to you, because of your severe siftings; believe that His heart is infinitely more so, who Himself is INCARNATE LOVE, and who became incarnate for this among other ends, that being sifted too, he might be able to sympathise and to succour (Heb. ii. 17, 18; iv. 15, 16).

CHAPTER XXX.

MANIFOLD TEMPTATIONS.

IN jotting down a few reflections suggested by the story of Hezekiah's temptation and fall (2 Chron. xxxii. 24–31), I am reminded that these narratives of Holy Scripture are given us for our warning, our instruction, and our comfort. They are told us, not for Hezekiah's sake, or Abraham's sake only, but for ours also (Rom. iv. 23, 24); and they are told us, not to entertain us with old histories, but that we may know more about God — about His thoughts and purposes towards us ; and more about ourselves, our natural tendencies and our dangers; and that, appropriating and applying to our own case the grand principles illustrated to us by the narratives, we may be forewarned and forearmed. Ofttimes the subjects of these narratives had to pay dearly for the lessons learned by them through their costly experiences; but we, if we be wise, may secure for ourselves the benefits of the same lessons without having to pay so dearly for them.   For God continues ever unchangeably the same, and man is everywhere the same, and the methods by which God leads souls out of nature, through grace, towards glory, are, in all their essential points, the same; and so, when the mere accidents of these Bible stories are stripped off, their vital points are being repeated over and over again in the experience of every one of us.

There is scarcely any subject of Divine revelation which is less familiar to the thoughts of most of us than the subject of temptation; though there are few subjects in which we have a deeper interest, or which are being more closely interwoven into the texture of our daily living.   We are all of us (I speak of Christians) undergoing temptation, we are continually undergoing it; indeed, we may each one speak of our present life as our Lord spoke of His, and call it "my temptation" (Luke xxii. 28). And there is the most indispensable necessity that we be thus subjected to all this "fiery trial" (1 Peter iv. 12).   Whatever of grace there may be in any of us, or whatever of evil, both of these have been developed into their present forms and measures, under the pressure of continually recurring temptation. And so solemn are its issues, so inconceivably vast are the interests which are being affected by the sifting process, that, if we would only look steadily at them for a little, the sight would either sink us into despair, or send us to the throne of grace with groanings which could not be uttered.

But though we too often forget the whole subject, our Lord in His teachings has not overlooked it ; and, better still, He does not forget or overlook ourselves as being ofttimes sorely tempted. As He foresaw Satan's sifting of Peter and of the others, and at once proceeded to provide against the danger (Luke xxii. 32) ; so equally still He foresees the danger and arranges for the safe keeping of every unit of His flock. And He has taught us to watch and pray for ourselves ; " Watch and pray that ye enter not into temptation." In the very brief model prayer given to us, this subject occupies a prominent place. If " the Lord's Prayer " consist of only six petitions, one of these is taken up with temptation ; but if there be seven petitions in it (as many think), no fewer than two out of the seven are appropriated to this very serious matter. The healthy Christian will listen to his Master's

2:18

words, and will seek to give the subject the same
prominence in his spiritual meditations which it
has in Holy Scripture.

The most cursory glance over Hezekiah's history
shows us that this was not the first of the good
man's trials.   He had been once and again severely
tested in the furnace of *affliction*, and he had stood
such testing well.   But God will now subject him
to a much more searching trial—the trial of
prosperity.   Ah, there are few who safely pass
through this.   Men can less easily endure to be
flattered and admired than to be despised and
ill-treated ; and so, in view of this, we see that the
best treatment which the world can give us (that is,
the treatment that is *safest* for ourselves) is her
hatred and cruel scorn.

Indeed, in his adversity, Hezekiah furnished an
admirable pattern to every suffering disciple.   Like
not a few of the Lord's children, his devout spirit
was at its best when his outward circumstances
were at the worst.   His sorrows sent him to his
knees before God ; but no sooner do flattering
seductions begin to influence him, than he lifts up
his heart in dangerous pride.   And it makes the
sin all the darker, that great part of the foundation on which he raised his self-glorification was

purely spiritual—was God's goodness to him in answering his cry in extremity. For pride can erect her towering superstructures on the most unsuitable foundations, or even without any foundation at all. We see to what heights of pride the Pharisees climbed by means of their unusual religiousness; we read of Jerusalem rejoicing in her pride, and being haughty because of God's holy mountain (Zeph. iii. 11). And most impressive warning of all, we hear the holy apostle confess that he needed to be subjected to peculiarly humbling discipline, needed even the messenger of Satan to buffet him, lest he should be exalted above measure by the very visions and voices seen and heard by him in the third heaven (2 Cor. xii. 1–7).

Some one might perhaps ask, "Wherein lay the wrong of which Hezekiah was now guilty? What evil had he done?" Well, Hezekiah had done nothing wrong, if we are to limit our conception of *sin* (as many do) to what is *vicious* or *criminal*. In this view of the case, Hezekiah was guilty of no sin, for he had done injury to no human interest. But there may be much *sin* where there is no *crime;* and so the king, while free from crime in this matter, was guilty of grievous sin against God. He had been indulging vanity, self-con-

fidence, and pride; and we see from the story
how severely God judged him for his *crimeless sin*,
and how heavily He chastened him for it.

And we, in our day of present trial, have the
same God to deal with.   True, though He Himself
remains unchanged, His methods of dealing with us
are considerably changed, but the change is *to the
severer side*.   The dispensation under which we
live is much more spiritual.   We are told in
Ps. xi. 5, that "the Lord trieth the righteous."
The same psalm assures us that the Lord Himself
is righteous, and that as the righteous Lord He
loveth righteousness.   But though infinitely righteous Himself, and infinitely loving righteousness,
His invariable method of treating the righteous is
—He severely tries them.   Yes, *severely;* as the
strongly figurative expression is meant to indicate,
"His eyes behold, His eyelids try."   He searches
Jerusalem with lighted candles (Zeph. i. 12).   He
"proves," He "visits," He "tries" every one of
His people (Ps. xvii. 3).   He "sets His heart" on
the doing of it; and He does it "every morning,"
nay, "every moment" (Job vii. 17, 18).

In Hezekiah's case, the trial is ascribed directly
to the Lord.   And many of our trials come
immediately from Him.   It was so with Abraham's

(see Gen. xxii. 1). But they are no less from Him when He makes use of instruments, and chooses to operate on us through the medium of others. He permitted Satan to tempt David ; but after all it was God's temptation (*i.e.*, trial) of His servant; and so the temptation is ascribed to God in one passage, and to Satan in another (2 Sam. xxiv. 1 ; 1 Chron. xxi. 1). We see from Job's case that Satan can do nothing against the saints without the explicit permission of God; while we see from the experience of the Lord Jesus that God in His trial of the righteous makes constant use of Satan; for no sooner had the Holy Spirit descended on our Saviour in a bodily form, than He led the Sinless One into the wilderness, to be there tempted of the devil (Mark i. 12).

And we do not look at our trials in the right light unless we recognise them as all coming to us, more or less directly, from the hands of God. Our eyes may see merely some attractive but forbidden enjoyment, while behind this bait for our lust, the old serpent is actively operating—whether we discern him or not—lusting more eagerly to compass our ruin than our excited desires are craving the seductive but forbidden sweet. But it is well to remember that as Satan lurks behind the attractive object, so God is actively operative behind him; and just as really as the enemy is using the tempting object for *his* ends, our Heavenly Father is watchfully superintending the whole, and is making use of Satan, and of his action on us, to accomplish His own higher ends.   Without Divine permission, the tempter could not operate at all; and this permission is so indispensable, that in a very intelligible sense God Himself is said to make the temptation which assails us, as well as to make the way of escape from it (1 Cor. x. 13).   Therefore, it is to Him that we pray " Lead us not into temptation," as the whole matter lies in His Sovereign hands.   As some one has said, " While Satan is watching me, it is my comfort to know that Christ is watching Satan."

In regard to the action ascribed to God in this trial of Hezekiah, we must not force an interpretation on the words which would contradict the analogy of the teaching of Holy Scripture.   It is affirmed that " *God left him*, to try him, that He might know all that was in his heart," not that God withdrew from Hezekiah any degree of grace already enjoyed by him, but only that He suffered him to enter on the trial *just as he was*, with all his natural tendencies to evil, and all his graciously acquired tendencies to good. The Lord merely stood aloof, as it were, and, unsolicited, refrained from ministering sufficient help to overcome the temptation. Had Hezekiah been duly aware of his own helpless weakness, he would have asked, and would, doubtless, have received the needed help ; as, indeed, he had ofttimes asked and received before. But, being in the spiritual condition in which he was, it was better for him that he should be tried, and that he should learn through his consequent fall, how very weak he was, and how completely dependent on the preserving grace of God.

But it is time that we should hastily gather a few practical lessons, and conclude.

1. Let the Christian count on meeting trial so long as he shall remain on earth. There is an urgent *need-be* that it should be so. The most wise and loving purposes of God respecting him demand his frequent trial. His present circumstances secure his constant trial. So far as he feels and walks as a Christian he lives as a dutiful child of God ; but he has to do so in a world which is in active rebellion against God, and which has the devil as its prince and its god. Nay, more, he has in him the sinless seed of God (1 John iii. 9),

by virtue of which he is a child of God; and yet this new nature is held in strangely intimate connection with a fallen nature, which cannot, *cannot* be subject to the law of God (Rom. viii. 7). Belonging to one world—the heavenly, he yet lives in another—the fallen earthly; how, then, can he escape the fiery trial? And, like Hezekiah's, his last trials may be the most dangerous. Even the want of outward trial may itself become a temptation, as many aged disciples feel who are passing quietly through the "Indian summer" which closes their year of earthly life. Like Bunyan's pilgrims, when they had almost completed their journey, these pilgrims are passing through the dangers of the enchanted ground, on which one is tempted to lie down and sleep.

2. Let the Christian not only expect to be tried, but to be severely tried. The Lord proportions the degree of trial to the strength of the individual (1 Cor. x. 13); and, if we have been really growing, we should be able in our riper years to endure a severer strain. There may be before some of us a sharper trial than any hitherto experienced—testing of our gold, as it were, amid the fierce fervours of the smelting-furnace.

We profess that we have given up our own wills,

that we have repented of the great sin of living to ourselves, that we have solemnly laid our entire selves (including all our belongings) as a living sacrifice on that altar, from which it is a sacrilege to resume any portion of such an offering. We affirm that we are dead with Christ, and that now, as risen with Him, we seek only the things which are above, that, like the hero-saints of Hebrews xi., we walk by faith and not by sight. All this we avow ; and nothing is more certain than that God is daily trying, and shall yet further try the sincerity of our profession. Many, alas ! are so blind that they discern not how completely their profession is condemned by the sad evidences which this continual testing elicits. Like Laodicea, they know not how poor they are.

3. Let the tried Christian count confidently on victory and increased blessing if he be only believing and faithful (James i. 12). How tenderly our Lord sympathises with His little ones during the whole process of life-long trial, and how efficiently He can sustain, no tongue of angel could express. Indeed, one of His reasons for living as " Man of Sorrows," was that He might be able fully to sympathise with His tried disciples, and to succour them perfectly (Heb. ii. 17 ; iv. 15, 16). Let us

comfort our hearts by the faith of His love; let us hide from danger under the protection of His Almighty arm. If we do, Satan can no more harm us by his power than he can harm Christ. It is not so much his power, but his *wiles*, that make his assaults dangerous; and even these cannot injure us if we receive his fiery darts on the shield of faith. He is the strong man armed, but our Keeper is stronger than he; and, having bruised His enemy under His own feet, He means to perfect His triumph by bruising him also under ours.

More than conquerors. What a wonderful word! It is not a mere victory that is secured to us—it is a triumph. And it is not a single victory, won through grace, once for all, but our life-long warfare has in it a daily battle and a daily conquest. The most terrific struggle ever carried on in the universe is that which is being waged between Christ's little ones and Christ's enemy; and the grandest victory to be won by creatures is that which is being achieved by Christ's might through Christ's members. The assailant, though so mighty, shall be more than conquered; and the assailed, so feeble in themselves, shall be more than conquerors.

4. But let the tried disciple remember that all his strength lies in Christ alone. Apart from Him the disciple can do NOTHING (John xv. 5). If, like Hezekiah or Peter, he meet the enemy in his own strength, the Lord will leave him to his own strength, in order to cure his unbelieving self-conceit. And, in his own strength, the strongest saint is no more a match for Satan than the suckling babe would be for an experienced Goliath. On the other hand, however weak we are, we cannot be too feeble for Christ's triumphant use of us. And He shall use us, only we must be believing and faithful.

But oh, the reluctance of the human heart to live by faith !—to be nothing in ourselves, and to have nothing of our own, but to seek and find all our joy, our wisdom, our strength, our everything, our very life even, only in Christ ! The young Christian sometimes wonders at the strange reluctance of the sinner to close with an offered Christ in simple faith. But the experienced Christian wonders much more at a still stranger fact—at his own stubborn and most sinful reluctance to live a life of faith on the Son of God. Every hour of every day our Lord might say to most of us : "O fool, and slow of heart to believe " !

" Watch and pray " ! " Watch and pray " !   Let these parting words of our Lord ring continually in our ears ; let us press them on ourselves and on our fellow disciples as we pass along !   How often, alas, is the story of Bunyan's pilgrims at Bypath Meadow repeated !   The road to heaven is always straight and narrow (rather *afflicted*) ; and therefore when an easier road, much easier to the flesh, presents itself, we are tempted to prefer it.   The main point of the temptation lies in the fact that the easier road seems to lie so perfectly parallel to the painful one, and that we seem to be able to reach our point quite as readily by the one road as by the other. Unless, then, our eye be single, and unless our spirit be strung to thorough self-denial, we shall almost certainly choose Bypath Meadow ; and if we do, bitter sorrow lies before us.   At the very least we shall find our way into the dungeons of Doubting Castle.

Let us settle it with ourselves as a finally accepted principle, that self-seeking and self-confidence can only lead us into evil.   And let us have it also for another settled principle, that if, unhappily, we should fall, there is no need even then to despair. There are *no depths so deep*—NO DEPTHS SO DEEP —out of which if we cry to God through Christ, the fallen man shall not be delivered. Jonah fell, well-nigh as far as man could fall, and yet his cry out of the belly of the fish was heard most graciously. Peter fell, and Hezekiah fell, but they also repented, and their stories are told us in the Book of God, not only to warn us lest we too should fall, but equally to encourage us, if unhappily we should.

> " He sitteth o'er the water floods,
>   Who once in days of old,
> Sank 'neath their depths, when o'er His head
>   The waves and billows rolled ;
> Yea, all the billows passed o'er Him,
>   Our sins, they brought Him low ;
> For us He met the vengeful storm—
>   He died, but liveth now.
>
> " And now He sitteth o'er the floods,
>   O'er Him they flow no more ;
> He lives, beyond the reach of storm,
>   On heaven's own peaceful shore ;
> And every tempest-driven bark,
>   With Jesus for its guide,
> Will soon be moored in harbour calm,
>   With Jesus to abide."

CHAPTER XXXI.

STEWARDSHIP.

" Moreover it is required in stewards, that a man be found
faithful."—1 Cor. iv. 2.

NEXT to the solemn question of a man's
personal salvation, the gravest matter to
which any one can turn his attention is that which
concerns his individual responsibility to God.
Wonder is often expressed that the careless sinner
can continue to overlook the *first* question ; is it
not just as wonderful that the *average* Christian
overlooks the *second ?*   Old John Chrysostom, quoting the inspired words of Heb. xiii. 17, "They watch
for your souls, as they THAT MUST GIVE ACCOUNT,"
says : " The awe of this warning excites my soul
continually."   And the Apostle Paul in giving his
dying charges to Timothy, his son, places him with
great solemnity under the same awful motives
(2 Tim. iv. 1, 2), " I charge thee," etc.

Stewardship resembles ownership in some superficial respects ; but they differ in this, that while the owner is responsible to none for his manner of employing the goods under his hand, seeing they are his own, the steward is a mere trusted servant appointed to administer certain goods belonging to another, and which, for this end, the owner of them has intrusted to him. He is therefore responsible for the faithful execution of his trust. If he forgets his responsibility, and if he presume to act *as if he were the owner*, instead of being merely the steward, then he EMBEZZLES his trust, and commits the gravest offence possible for one in his position.

In the verses (1 Cor. iv. 1, 2) it is plain that Paul's present reference is to gospel ministry; however, for sake of general profiting, we may extend the principle announced, and apply it so as to comprehend *everything* that can be included *within the province of a Christian's life*. Every Christian is a steward of the manifold grace of God (1 Peter iv. 10).

And if it be asked, What is it in respect to which we are to account ourselves trusted stewards, and of which we shall soon have to give account to God ? the answer is a very startling one. Our stewardship includes OURSELVES, and ALL that we *are*, ALL that we have. There is NOTHING in our hands of which God is not

exclusive owner; and of which we are any more
than mere responsible stewards. Our very *persons*
are not our own, for we have been bought with a
price; and this "that we may glorify God in our
bodies, and in our spirits, which are God's" (1 Cor.
vi. 19, 20). "Every bodily power, every mental
faculty, every capacity of affection, and all these to
be always exercised at their highest strain" (Matt.
xxii. 37). ALL a Christian's time, every single
moment of it; ALL his money, every single farthing
of it; ALL his influence, every possible shred of it—
these belong to God, and the man, as a steward, is
to expend them faithfully for his Lord. So far as
we fail to do so, we *embezzle*. Oh! if this were
recognised worthily (and why should it not be so?)
the meanest place in all the Church would be seen
to afford ample scope for the faithfulness of an
angel.

Note well, then, the two facts: EVERY Christian
is a steward; and his stewardship includes EVERY-
THING belonging to Him.

And the passage teaches us that the first
indispensable of a "good steward" (1 Peter iv. 10),
is that "he be found FAITHFUL." We so constantly
forget this; and in our heedlessness we admire in
others, or we covet for ourselves, mere amount of

intrusted material. We think it well (of itself), to be rich in money, and gifted in mind, and of vigorous health, and of extensive influence; forgetting that, unless with all these be joined a proportionate FAITHFULNESS, they only go towards making the final reckoning the more dreadful.

Yes, faithfulness is the *first* thing to be aimed at—PERFECT faithfulness.

Not even SUCCESS, but faithfulness. Many a faithful saint has but a small measure of apparent success; while sometimes an unfaithful servant seems to carry all before him. No matter, the Lord shall assign to every man his own reward, not according to tangible results, but according to his OWN LABOUR (1 Cor. iii. 8).

Faithfulness, even before *wisdom* in the choice of proper methods. Nay, in a steward, faithfulness and wisdom are the same; to be perfectly faithful is to be perfectly wise (see Luke xii. 42). The Lord crowns the *faithful* servant as the GOOD servant (Matt. xxv. 21–23).

And there is much more involved in being a faithful steward than occurs to one to think of, at first glance. We are to use EVERYTHING that we have ALWAYS, and only for the *highest* glory of God, and for the *best* good of *every* one of our fellow-

2:19

men, even to our eating and our drinking, as well as to every other act besides ; all that we do should be done to God's glory, and for man's edification (1 Cor. x. 31 ; 2 Cor. xii. 19). Such a style of living shall leave us no surplus whatever to expend on self-indulgence, or self-pleasing ; and, therefore, whatever is so expended is simply *embezzled* (Rom. xv. 1–3). In fact, if we set ourselves to follow Christ, and the apostles, and the devotedly faithful in all ages, we shall aim at having our lives pitched on a key which shall look like insanity to the eyes of average professors.

We must not allow ourselves to overlook the need of *perfect* faithfulness, in the discharge of our heavenly trust, by the fact that our service may lie very much among small and apparently trifling matters,—so small that our pride is tempted to judge them beneath our care. No mistake could be more fatal ! It is these very trifles (so deemed) which God appoints us as our special service to Him, and it is by means of our faithful attention to these very trifles that our love to Himself shall be estimated. It is by means of these trifles (if at all) that the crown of glory is to be won. And be it remembered, the smaller the sphere of service, the more beautifully shines the faithfulness which devotes itself heartily to it. Two mites, which make but one farthing, seemed so small a gift in the eyes of the holder of them, that she was ashamed to give them; but because her faithfulness was so great, while yet her gift was small, see how gloriously it was commended.

On the other hand, the slothful servant in Matt. xxv. 18, feeling his one talent to be but a trifle, did nothing with it, and was condemned, not for small gift, but for *unfaithfulness*.

For though in this stage of God's dealings with sinful men, *grace* deals with the sinner in a way quite apart from any full display of *judgment* (John xii. 47), yet, at the close, the final judgment shall be in pure and holy righteousness (Acts xvii. 31). And the crown of glory assigned to faithful stewards shall be a crown of righteousness, which shall be assigned by One who acts as Righteous Judge (2 Tim. iv. 8). It is but a sixpence then; and yet it is quite certain that my expenditure of this sixpence shall influence, favourably or unfavourably, my own whole eternity; and it may also prove to be the turning-point of eternal life for some fellow-man.

In view of all this, let us hastily consider a few practical lessons :—

1. Since so much turns on my faithfulness to God's intrusted gift, and since I find my heart naturally so self-seeking, so unbelieving, and so unfaithful, how needful that I PRAY more than hitherto for this indispensable grace of perfect faithfulness, and let me see that I do so with that IMPORTUNITY to which God never refuses the graces of His Holy Spirit (Luke xi. 8–13).

2. Discontent with my lot is out of the question. With my faithfulness as it is, what if my lot were to be more favourable, as it is called? In this case, I should only be acting the unfaithful steward on a bigger scale, and turning the good gifts of God, which He meant for my blessing, into a curse.

3. And anything like PRIDE is still further out of the question. That gift, whatever it may be, is not mine, but God's. He has trusted it to me, moreover, not for my own sake, but for sake of other weak ones, who need the help of it; and to whom, therefore, it belongs more really than it does to me. I am, in the exercise of my gift, not their superior, but their servant for Jesus' sake (2 Cor. iv. 5). God in His grace *to them* meant its final benefits to reach them, through my faithful use of it; therefore He intrusted the expenditure of it to

me. And if I fail to be faithful—faithful to God, and faithful to them, I am a thief and a robber, robbing not only *from* God, but *from my fellow-man*. And if my possession of any gift be puffing me up, this fact is proof that I am not faithful ; I am forgetting both the purpose for which I have been trusted with it, and the strict—most strict account which I shall yet have to make of my faithfulness in discharging it.

4. Let us on no account permit ourselves to be easily satisfied with low and common measures of faith, or of faithfulness; God expects us to grow in both, and He will be displeased with us if we do not. We are not living spiritually if we are not growing. It is solemn to see how God severely chastens for unbelief, acts which had in them a great deal of faith. This faith, however, was not according to the measure that might be looked for from the person, and so, he is not commended for the faith, but censured for the unbelief. Take Moses, for instance, in Numbers xx. See him visited with no less than death for his unbelief, while yet the very unbelieving act exhibits a faith that is truly wonderful. Let us remember that it is not enough that we be believing and faithful so far; but our faith and faithfulness should be proportionate to

our experience and responsibilities. And it certainly is not so, if the habitual sense of our responsibility be not always felt as most deeply solemn.

5. Let us often advert to this question, in a spirit of deepest earnestness, and with hearty prayer for Divine help. It is *heedlessness* which more than anything else keeps Christian souls in their low degrees of faith and faithfulness. Every passing hour is telling gravely on our present character and our eternal destiny. Let us ask ourselves often, "How did the last hour tell on me?" Did I make use of it to get nearer to God in true communion, to procure at His throne of grace the maximum attainable by me of spiritual power? And what have I done for others? Is there likely to be another jewel in my crown, because of this last hour? Or have I spent it so that its final issues are like to be altogether different? Let us often examine ourselves as to this point, that we may give *daily* account to Christ our Lord, to whom ere long we shall have to give strict account, when the life-long day of service here is over.

6. And whatever the past may have been, whether the review be one of wasted time and marred blessing, or of hearty improvement of them

both, let nothing hinder us from setting our faces like a flint to the most perfect faithfulness possible to us now. There is nothing so certain as that God will help us, if in obedient faith and self-denial we decide to be faithful to Him. He cannot fail the faithful, trusting soul ; but if a man continue to loiter because he feels weak and impotent, expecting the influx of a strength which shall lift him out of the place of humble trust, he expects what God never promised, while yet he continues to be unfaithful to what God has already given. Begin at once, and let the language of our heart be :—

> " Take my life, and let it be
> Consecrated, Lord, to Thee ;
> Take my moments and my days,
> Let them flow in ceaseless praise.

> " Take my hands, and let them move
> At the impulse of Thy love ;
> Take my feet, and let them be
> Swift and beautiful for Thee.

> " Take my voice, and let me sing
> Always, only, for my King ;
> Take my lips and let them be
> Filled with messages for Thee.

> " Take my silver and my gold ;
> Not a mite would I withhold ;
> Take my intellect, and use
> Every power as Thou shalt choose.

"Take my will, and make it Thine ;
   It shall be no longer mine ;
   Take my heart, it is Thine own,
   It shall be Thy royal throne.

"Take my love ; my Lord I pour
   At Thy feet its treasure store ;
   Take myself, and I will be
   Ever, only, ALL for Thee."

CHAPTER XXXII.

CHRISTIAN SERVICE.

1. The Weak Things.

THE Lord not only graciously condescends to work with the feeblest instruments—men or things—but He *prefers* to do so. He "chooses"; see the repetition of this word so frequently in 1 Cor. i. 27, 28. Oh, to be ever *weak* ENOUGH for His gracious use of us! It is in service precisely as it is in the matter of a sinner's first reception. God's grace in Christ Jesus is so free, so purely gratuitous, that no fancied merit of ours, and no fancied capacity for serving, can attract His favour to us in the slightest degree; while this grace is also so abundant and so readily bestowed, that our unworthiness and our feebleness cannot hinder it in the least.

2. He took upon Him the form of a Servant.

How deeply striking! more so than I can find words to express, when I see the blessed Son of God working in a Galilean carpenter's shed till He was thirty years of age. Think of WHO He was, think of His sole errand here, think of the condition of the men and women everywhere around Him; and then think of Him going on quietly from week to week, and year to year, planing and sawing His rough boards.

Till the Father calls He does nothing. Christ's time was the Father's time; and the Father's time was not yet come. As for religious men generally (alas, too many Christians are to be included) the words of John vii. 6 are applicable, "My time is not yet come, but YOUR TIME IS ALWAYS READY." Yes. Always ready, for the self-willed worker has his times in his own self-willed keeping; and after the manner of the wicked king of the last days, they "do according to their own will" (see Daniel xi. 16, 36). OUR calling is to "do the WILL OF GOD" and nothing else; and for this we ever need much faith and patience (Heb. x. 36); and also much self-denial.

3. OPPORTUNITIES.

OPPORTUNITIES given to us in providence for service are God's call to us. Slothful servants neglect them. Moderately faithful servants improve them readily and diligently. But single-hearted and devoted servants not only improve such available opportunities, but go on to create opportunities when they do not find them; not in the energy of self-will and self-reliance, but in the activity of a faith that sees the solemnities of the Invisible, and of a love that cannot rest. The Lord grant to all His own a fresh anointing EVERY DAY.

---

4. THE WILL OF GOD.

WE ought never to forget that meantime our true work is day by day to do or to bear THE WILL OF GOD, in the strength received from God. We have to do this, ONLY THIS, and neither more nor less. How *easy* to do it, and yet how *hard.* Easy, if all SELF-WILL were utterly exterminated, and the fleshly mind, like a conquered enemy, were kept bruised under one's feet. But HARD, inasmuch as self-will, slain apparently yesterday, is alive and active to-day; and fleshly wisdom, cast out under its name of fleshly wisdom, assumes the name and disguise of some heavenly grace, and is permitted, like Hushai the Archite, to spoil our counsels. And yet our gracious God is overruling all, and is causing everything to work together for good. God has His own wise and beautiful plan for us; but that perfect plan is HIS, not *ours*. As for us, we have at best the most glimmering conception of it. Meanwhile, our place is to exercise perfect faith and perfect faithfulness.

---

5. "COME YE YOURSELVES APART."

IT is not favourable to true health of soul—any more than it is to the body—to be too continually engrossed with details of even most important service. We need the "Come ye yourselves apart and rest awhile" of Mark vi. 31; nay, when this cannot be had, we need the "rising up a great while before day" for solitary prayer, as in Mark i. 35. May the gracious Lord sweeten our seasons of retirement with much of His own presence. And in this way, renew our strength for service (Isaiah xl. 31).

---

6. FAITHFULNESS.

WE have little to do with success—that belongs to the Lord; but we have everything to do with faithfulness—it is that which is required and expected at our hands. The one grand point indispensable in a steward is that "he bo found FAITHFUL" (1 Cor. iv. 2). It is the faithfulness of the steward that constitutes him a *good* servant ; and it is the want of faithfulness that makes him *wicked* (Matthew xxv. 21, 23, 26). Oh, to be faithful, whether the trust be little or much ; and again, oh, to be faithful !

We ought also to be infinitely more anxious about the QUALITY of our work than about its QUANTITY. If the quality be all right there is no fear that the quantity will fall short. The grace that secures the one will secure the other.

---

7. " CAST THY BREAD UPON THE WATERS."

IT is a cause for real deep thankfulness, any little encouragement graciously vouchsafed in connection with work for the Lord. It is both pleasant and stimulating ; but after all the true sower must cast his bread on the waters in simple faith, seeing nothing, but trusting God for the unseen issues. The true work of a true worker shall never be in vain (1 Cor. xv. 58).

Our Divine Lord Himself, since He became the Father's servant, had to act on this principle of dependence and of faith (see Isa. xlix. 1–6, especially ver. 4). In every respect He committed His cause simply and absolutely to Him who judgeth righteously (1 Peter ii. 23), in this leaving us an example (ver. 21).

---

8. " THE GLORY OF CHRIST."

WHAT a wonderful expression which Holy Scripture applies to the Lord's true servants; they are " THE GLORY OF CHRIST " (2 Cor. viii. 23). What a word to apply to dust and ashes. Such a thought could never have entered into the heart of man to conceive, had it not been most graciously made known to us by the Holy Spirit in the Word.

---

9. "To Watch for Souls."

How very solemn it is to deal with an immortal soul, especially when one feels his own incompetency. I don't wonder at all at Paul's words, "I was with you in weakness, and IN FEAR, and IN MUCH TREMBLING" (1 Cor. ii. 3).

It is a very solemn thing to place one's-self in Christ's hands for service ; "to WATCH FOR SOULS," and at the same time to do so as one who feels that he shall soon have to "give account" (see Heb. xiii. 17).

---

10. God's Guidance Indispensable.

How indispensable is *His guidance* for happy service, and such as will be acceptable to God. Folly seems to reign everywhere. Wisdom is the exception. And yet the Blessed Lord (Luke xvi. 8) suggests to us that, as the children of light, we are not even on a level with the foolish world in respect to wisdom. They in *their* special sphere are really wiser than we are *in ours*. Stupid and blundering as is the wisdom of the poor demented world in the world's own things, *our* OWN WISDOM, as spiritual men, is still more stupid and blundering in our judgment and treatment of spiritual things. How very humiliating is an assurance like this ; but how needful that we know the fact, lest we should trust to *our* OWN WISDOM, instead of trusting to His guidance who is "Christ the wisdom of God," and who has been made of God to us, "wisdom" and all besides (1 Cor. i. 24–30). Satan would desire nothing better of us than that we should set ourselves to serve God in *our own* strength, and following *our own* wisdom, and seeking *our own* self-exaltation.

---

11. "THE TIME IS SHORT."

THE season of the year reminds us that we too are passing away. What our hands find to do in His service let us do it with our might, for our time to do it may be very limited. And since our Lord has gone into heaven, let our affections go with Him. And then when He returns He shall take up our persons with Him as now our hearts. Enduring patiently, labouring faithfully, loving fervently, waiting expectantly. And all this because of a faith which receives and rests upon all our Heavenly Father's uttered words—this is our attitude as the servants, as well as the members of Christ.

12. " My Times are in Thy Hand."

WHATEVER be our circumstances, we can say " My times are in Thy hand " (Ps. xxxi. 15), times of weakness as of vigour ; and all are arranged in unerring wisdom and in infinite love. And when self-will is given up, and we are content to be pleased with whatever pleases God, then one thing is as delightful as another ; for in this case " the gladness of our joy " is in God Himself, and not in circumstances. Then as for service, that is a very simple matter. We can always serve God by yield-ing ourselves up to His holy will, and we cannot serve Him at all otherwise ; and so, if our spirits be right, our mere circumstances can never hinder

2:20

either our service or our enjoyment. " Behold, to OBEY is better than *sacrifice ;* and to hearken than the fat of rams " (1 Sam. xv. 22).

---

13. ABLE TO PLEASE GOD.

WHAT an inexpressibly sweet thought it is to a loving heart to know that, poor and worthless and sinful as I am, I can give pleasure to my GOD. Once we could not do this, for " they that are in the flesh cannot please God " (Rom. viii. 8) ; but now having been regenerated, made one with Christ, and dwelt in by the Holy Spirit, we are both able to please God, and are also responsible for doing it. What a powerful motive this should be. What a constant spur in our sides. What a source of strength in self-denial. What an encouragement in service. Since we can give pleasure to God, shall we grudge to do it—we who owe Him ALL, we to whom He is our EVERYTHING ? True, we may not be able to honour Him by any great work, or striking service, but we may give Him pleasure in our care to serve Him in the little works which He puts into our hands.

14. SELF-CONTROL.

SOME Christians are gifted by nature with uncommonly strong and vehement emotions and passions ; excellent gifts if under strong control, and that instead of using the whip they tighten the bridle.

CHAPTER XXXIII.

SANCTIFIED AFFLICTION.

1. God's School.

I AM getting more in love with suffering—not certainly for its own sake, for there is nothing that is lovable about it; but can anything be so sweet as to suffer at the perfect will of God, in the company of the Lord Jesus, and with the Blessed Spirit actually rendering the suffering effective? Oh, yes, the severe and heavy cross, willingly borne, is God's grand ordinance for putting us in actual possession of many of His most precious mercies. Through it, He imparts to us measures of strength and joy, of humility and patience, vigour of faith and liveliness of hope, such as we receive nowhere else. It is under the Cross that we enjoy the most delightful communion with the Man of Sorrows. Christ has been appointed to be our sole Prophet, our only Teacher; and He teaches in the

school of affliction.   How many of the glorified
have been taught almost all they ever learned at
this school.   It was here David was educated, and
Job, and Moses, and Joseph, and Jeremiah, and
Paul.   Nay, the Blessed Lord Himself was for
long a pupil in this school; for though He was a
Son, yet it was here that He learned obedience by
the things which He suffered (see Heb. v. 8).   Oh,
they are indeed blessed souls, whom God enters as
pupils in this school (Ps. xciv. 12); but trebly
happy are they who are kept long enough in it till
their training is complete.

One of the services which affliction renders is
this—it forces the soul out of the region of shadows
and talk, into the region of realities.   We have
such a tendency to rest in mere shadows, that,
while the religion of the formal is made up of
shadows, even that of the true Christian has far too
much of the shadowy in it at times, and too little
of the solid.

But God sends some severe affliction; and these
shadows flee away.   The affliction does to the
religious man's fine sentiments what a rough shake
does to the dream of the sleeper.   Oh, then,
nothing, NOTHING will serve his need, or sustain his
fainting soul, but solid, Divine REALITIES; and

these known in the actual EXPERIENCE of them.
He must, as it were, look upon with his eyes, and
his hands must handle of the Word of Life. He
would sink if he could not see, and hear, and
taste, and touch, and smell the things of the
spiritual world. He must look into the tender,
melting eyes of Jesus; must feel the soft touch of
His grasping hand. As he leans his throbbing
head on his Saviour's bosom, he must hear the
gentle voice whispering in his ear: "Fear not, I
am beside thee; it is I who am doing all this to
thee, and doing it all in purest love—I who
bought thee with My life, and who am keeping
thee as the apple of Mine eye." Nay, more, the
sorely-tried man cannot be satisfied, unless he
feel lip laid to lip, and be thrilled to almost
unbearable raptures by the kisses of Immanuel's
mouth. Oh, how blessed is the affliction, however
heavy it may be, which necessitates communion of
this kind; a communion in which, though the
affliction continues to be as painful to heart and
flesh as ever, it loses every particle of bitterness
and grief.

2. CHRIST SUFFERED, LEAVING US AN EXAMPLE.

How easy would it have been for the Blessed Lord to have escaped His dreadful sufferings, if He had allowed the least self-will in Himself! He had only to pray His Father for angelic help, and the glorious hosts of heaven would have clustered round their adored Lord, and snatched Him at once from His murderous enemies. An absolute, unconditional prayer was all that was needed (see Matt. xxvi. 53, 54). But how could He pray that prayer—He who had come for the one end of doing the will of the Father, the whole will, and nothing else but only that blessed will ? He says, " How then shall the Scripture be fulfilled, that thus it MUST be ? " For, like us, He found His Father's will about Him in the Bible; and it was His MEAT to do that will, and to finish His appointed work (John iv. 34).

This will of His Father settled for Him every question ; and it was impossible that He could choose differently from what His Father had appointed, that is, from what Scripture had foretold of Him. But all this applies also to our-selves. In Scripture we learn what is the will of our Heavenly Father about us ; and, like our Lord, we are here to do, and to bear that holy will. The Bible foretells the sufferings of Christ's members, just as it foretold those of our glorious Head; and, if we be led by His Spirit, we shall no more seek exemption from the Cross than Jesus did. Infinitely better than exemption is the faith which rejoices in the Cross; nay, which is able to leap for joy (James i. 2, 3 ; Luke vi. 23).

---

3. How Affliction should be received.

There is often a very great difference between affliction as God gives it, and the same affliction as we receive it and make use of it. As God sends it, the affliction may in many respects be very severe, but it is always within suitable limits (1 Cor. x. 13), and when the sufferer is rightly exercised under it, it is always accompanied by abundant consolations. God sheds His very sweetest smiles on His most sorely-tried little ones. But when a man receives the chastisement in a spirit of self-will and unbelieving impatience, these make the burden almost beyond endurance. But then it was not God who laid that crushing burden on the man ; it was the man's own unbelief, which has multiplied tenfold the suffering which God appointed him. If I might use the simile, God's wounds are, every one of them, clean cuts with the lancet, and are meant to heal ; but if we foolishly rub them till they get inflamed and canker and grow into horrible ulcers, which are like to over-whelm us, the fault is wholly ours. And this last we shall do, unless, in humble faith, we commit ourselves to our trusted FATHER, that He may fulfil in us all the good pleasure of His goodness. Oh, may the God of all grace, able and willing to do far above our asking or our thinking, lead us ever nearer and nearer to Himself ; and this at whatever cost it may be to the flesh.

---

4. SICKNESS A GIFT FROM GOD.

SICKNESS is A GIFT from God, as well as *health ;* that is, it is a something that is actually *given.* Men speak as if health were alone the gift, and sickness were merely the withdrawal of the gift. But in truth sickness is as much a gift—a thing given—as health is. And it is also a LOVE GIFT—

a gift given to those whom God loves (John xi. 3), and because He loves them (Heb. xii. 6, 7). It is sent in the tenderest, most yearning, most considerate LOVE. More than this, it is a gift of love which sometimes we urgently need—so urgently need that we cannot dispense with it,—need it more than we need health and strength. And further still, it is often greatly blessed—more blessed than health had been, more blessed than health usually is, for the finest gold is always refined in the fiercest furnace. God's purpose about *one* beloved child of His is, that he be honoured with much laborious serving, and therefore He gives him the precious gift of strength, with His own blessing added to it ; but His purpose with *another* beloved child is, that he be exceedingly purified and refined, and therefore He sends him the precious gift of sore and lengthened affliction, puts him in fact into the very heart of the fire, and blows the glowing coals into a white heat by turning the bellows on them. And let me add that God may be, and often is, glorified *as much* by the sanctified sufferings of the one, as by the sanctified labours of the other; and men around are often as much helped by what they see in the one, as by what they hear from the other.

5. "Blessed is the Man whom Thou Chastenest."

While I feel very tenderly for you, it would be quite wrong to say that I am sorry that you should be called to suffer as you are now doing, for such a feeling would be dishonouring to our *God and Father*. It would be a shocking thing to say of any earthly father, that we were sorry for his children, because of his way of treating them; and neither you nor I think in this way of our most tenderly loving Father. Nay, we lie down in peace beneath His chastening hand, and we quiet our hearts by repeating to them His own words: "Blessed is the man whom Thou chastenest, and teachest him out of Thy law" (Ps. xciv. 12).

The severity of pain may be greatly mitigated, and its bitterness reduced, by our yielding up ourselves absolutely into the trusted hands of the infinitely loving Father, and by our ceasing to struggle against Him, even so far as to permit in our hearts the faintest wish for it to be otherwise with us than as He wills, but on the contrary that we CHOOSE it, and find in our suffering precious opportunities of glorifying and enjoying God. Faith enables us to do this where it is lively;

for it sees in the sufferings the wise and loving,
the lovely and beloved, WILL of God. It KNOWS,
with perfect certainty, that that will is working out
the very highest possible good for the child of His
love ; and, knowing this, it sings with glad and free
heart in the midst of the fires. No doubt, suffering
pain is a great trial to faith, yet we are called on
to believe the love in spite of the suffering ; nay,
that the suffering is sent by the purest, tenderest
love; nay, to realise it so vividly that it shall
sweeten the cup made up of mingled love and
suffering, so as to have no taste but sweetness.
Such faith does God ask and expect from you and
me (see James i. 2) ; nay, better still, such faith
does God give us.

6. "THE LORD IS VERY PITIFUL, AND OF
TENDER MERCY."

PITIFUL means full of pity ; and God is VERY
pitiful (Jas. v. 11), that is, VERY FULL of it. A
little suffices to fill your heart or mine ; but think
of what is needed to fill up the infinite capacity of
God's great heart—nay, to fill it VERY FULL. And
it is full ; nay, in addition to the pity, there is

mercy, and this mercy is said to be *tender mercy*.

And we need to be told by God Himself that it is so, for none of us would ever have found it out from what we see or experience of the bitterness of life in this world of breaking hearts. If we were merely to reason on what we see and feel of the sorrows and sufferings that so abound, we would scarcely think that God is pitiful *at all*, much less that He is *full*, VERY FULL of pity and of tender mercy. But we must not reason, we must believe, if we would know God aright. When a disease is sharp and dangerous, the very kindest of physicians is compelled to use sharp and painful remedies; and our disease of soul needs all the suffering inflicted on us.

When children are very foolish and stubborn, the most loving father has, from his love, to take up the rod to them ; and we, alas, are so stubborn and so foolish. When subjects are rebellious and lawless, the most pitiful of sovereigns cannot but deal severely with the rebels ; and this world is up in rebellion against God.

But, in spite of all misunderstood appearances, let us hold fast this truth that God is VERY, VERY full of pity. So pitiful is He that its greatness, its tenderness, are utterly incomprehensible to man. It is a love that passeth knowledge (Eph. iii. 18, 19). It takes an actual new birth before a man can believe it at all; and, even then, his faith in it is still mournfully imperfect. So great is it, that He prefers to give us a great blessing rather than a small one; and to bestow on us, when we can safely receive them, a hundred mercies rather than only one. What may we not count on from His pity, who became partaker of our most sorrowful life—but without sin—in order that, through His own experience of it, He might be the better able to pity us and to relieve us (Heb. ii. 17; iv. 15).

Let us seek to dwell much, and to dwell often, on this lovely aspect of God's character. The dread of God's wrath is often needed to waken up the careless, hard-hearted sinner from his slumbers, but it is the sweet enjoyment of His tender mercy that melts, and strengthens, and encourages the saint. It is the LOVE OF CHRIST which constrains us (see 2 Cor. v. 14). The ravishing contemplation of God's boundless love in Christ Jesus, and the delighted rest of heart and soul in it, will do a thousand times more to sanctify the believer than any amount of gloomy brooding over his own sins, or of gazing, as it were, into hell. At the same time, a deep and powerful conviction of the enormity of our personal guilt as sinners most sweetly combines with a strong faith in this marvellous Divine pity in drawing the heart to Jesus, and in helping to fix it firmly there.

And with what fearless confidence should we commit ourselves wholly to this very pitiful Lord. With what patience and loving resignation should we accept His chastisements, quite assured that He never afflicts willingly, but always for our profit (Heb. xii. 10). And if His treatment of us seems to be severe, let us see in this only the greatness of His pity, and the virulence of our sore disease which needs such treatment.

---

7. "ALL THINGS WORK TOGETHER FOR GOOD."

IF the Christian, even when under heavy affliction, may not be happy, who should? Since it is His privilege to look on all his circumstances, not with the eyes of fleshly wisdom, but with the eye of faith, and in the light of God. And what does he see? He sees all things working together for his good (Rom. viii. 28). He sees that the affliction, which unbelief and self-will count very, very heavy, is as light as a feather—not worthy to be named or thought of in comparison with the coming glory to which it leads (Rom. viii. 18). Nay, he sees that the same light affliction is actually working out the glory; so working it out, that for him this glory could not be without the prior affliction to work it out (2 Cor. iv. 17). He sees, besides, that this affliction is but for a moment—a little moment—while the glory which it is working for him is to be eternal. He sees, also, in every circumstance of his trial (every one) the hand of God busily working all, and arranging all, so as to secure his *very highest* blessing. And, in the meantime, looking at himself and his troubles in the light of God, and with the eyes of faith, he feels that, even now, his joys (his spiritual joys) are far more numerous and far more weighty than his few trifling temporary sorrows are. He wonders at his ever being downcast because of them, and remonstrates with himself, saying: "Why art thou cast down, O my soul, and why art thou disquieted in me? Still trust in God." He, therefore, congratulates himself, instead of lamenting his lot (as unbelief does); and he triumphantly exclaims:

" The lines are fallen unto me in pleasant places, I have a goodly heritage." He says to himself : The infinite God is mine, with all His unknown riches of grace and glory. He is my very Father. Christ is mine—nearer to me than my own body is to my own soul, and more full of love to me than all others besides. The Holy Spirit is mine— dwelling in me as in His temple, and this as my Comforter, my Guide, my Sanctifier. Heaven is mine, eternity is mine, the boundless universe is mine (see 1 Cor. iii. 21, 22; Rev. xxi. 7), for I am a child of God, therefore an heir of God, and a joint-heir with Christ (Rom. viii. 17). Should such an one as I then be downcast for a few days of trouble of any bodily kind ? Surely not, since GOD HIMSELF is my portion —" The Lord is the portion of mine inheritance, and of my cup " (Ps. xvi. 5). And when a man has such a portion, such a cup, he may sing all the days of his life, for his cup " RUNNETH OVER " (Ps. xxiii. 5).

---

8. " CASTING ALL OUR CARE ON HIM."

WE are strictly forbidden to burden ourselves with care about our earthly condition. It is a sin,

and it brings its punishment with it.   And what
an unspeakable privilege to be allowed to cast every
care on Him who is so caring for us.   I think I can
hear Him speaking to me in such words as these :
No mother ever loved so tenderly as I love thee ;
and no man ever looked after his own weightiest
concerns as I am, day and night, looking after thine.
Since thou gavest thyself up to Me, everything
that belongeth to thee is most precious in Mine
eyes.   Every hair on thy head is counted ; thy
tears, see, I have put them all in My bottle, for
I count them as treasures.   No enemy can possibly
hurt thee ; he that would touch thee would touch
the apple of Mine eye.   Oh, My little one, trust
Me more fully ; and above all else, abhor the
thought of taking thyself out of My hands—and
thou takest thyself out of My hands, as often as
thou beginnest to care for thyself, and to plan for
thyself, instead of leaving thy whole concerns to My
loving care.   Oh, how that foolish wisdom of thine
grieves Me !   Why wilt thou not believe My assurance to thee, that there are no interests in all the
universe that are more devotedly looked after than
I am looking after thine.   Nestle, then, more
trustingly and more lovingly in My bosom ; and
while I give thee for thy joy the assurance of My

infinite love to thee, do thou give Me in return the joy of seeing thee resting calmly, and sweetly trusting in My love.

---

9. God's Will and not Mine.

How inexpressibly sweet it is to ourselves, and how glorifying to God, to abandon ourselves without any reserve to His holy will. No service serves Him like this; and no joy is so delightful, so heavenlike as this. It was Christ's own service (Ps. xl. 8). It was Christ's own joy (John iv. 32, 34 ; Heb. xii. 2). He left us this service, this joy, as a legacy to us (John xiv. 27; xv. 11). Oh, let us prove ourselves heirs to it ; and what an easy yoke, what a light burden this is, when it is borne by faith and love (Matt. xi. 30). Oh, how delightful it is ! The happy man has nothing in his lot but what he is glad to have in it; and there is nothing wanting from his lot that he would rather should be in it; for he desires, and delights in, nothing save in the perfect, the wise, the sovereign will of God, and as that will of God is always carried out, the man's peace is actually perfect (Isa. xxvi. 3),

for he trusts himself UTTERLY to God. He lies
down at his Father's knee, and sleeps the soft sweet
sleep of *God's* beloved (Ps. iv. 8; Ps. cxxvii. 2).
For it is God's will that we should leave ourselves
to His all-perfect will, and in all circumstances
should heartily say, *"Thy will be done on earth
even as it is done in heaven."* If, then, He sees
best to withhold from us, or to remove from us,
something that the natural heart desires, we cheerfully let it go ; and if He lays on us some trying
burden from which the natural heart shrinks, we
say with our blessed Saviour, "The cup which my
Father hath given me, shall I not drink it ? " God
never sanctions self-will in His children. There is
no such thing as self-will in heaven ; and, therefore,
heaven is what it is, holy and happy. There is
nothing but self-will in hell; therefore hell is what
it is, the pit of horrors, the blackness of darkness.
And the believing man on earth is Christlike, holy,
and happy only in so far as, filled with the spirit
of his Master, he is in harmony with the will of
God, and then he proves that will always to be
good, and acceptable, and welcome.

> "Nought seek I here but to fulfil
> In life and death Thy lovely will."

10. God's Plan is the Best.

It is perfectly certain that God has a plan for all His suffering children, which plan is infinitely wise and infinitely loving. It includes EVERY *interest* and EVERY incident connected with each of them. The sufferer has his plan about his life and his service to the Lord, and it often seems that his plan is not exactly the same as God's ; and this may indeed be true, for OUR thoughts are seldom HIS. As heaven is higher than earth and God is greater than man, so His plan is always loftier and better than ours. Let us hasten to " Amen " His, and to reject our own. Nay, let us cease from the bad habit of forming any plan about ourselves at all, and, simply laying ourselves as consecrated victims on His holy altar (Rom. xii. 1), let us patiently await, *from day to day*, the unfolding of our Heavenly Father's majestic plans. This at least is certain, that Divine love, associated with unerring Divine wisdom, is doing ITS VERY BEST FOR US. Let us, in the assured faith of this, cast our own self-will from us as being virtually rebellion, and let us joyously, lovingly, say " Amen " to the holy, PERFECT will of God (Ps. xviii. 30). This does not in the least hinder us spreading our desires humbly and reverently before Him in prayer, but it secures our welcoming the answer to these prayers, WHATEVER IT MAY BE, and that we wait with patience for the answer, knowing that that affliction, which presses on us so heavily, was in all its details planned for us, and is being executed on us by the same infinite love which gave the Son of God to die for our sins.

----

11. No Will of our Own.

OH, my beloved friend, what an actual heaven upon earth it is to have NO WILL of our own, no choice of *anything*, but to lay ourselves wholly in our Father's loving hands, and to be pleased perfectly with whatever it pleases Him to appoint us; and what a hell on earth it is to be torn asunder and tormented with our own wishes to be this, and to have that, and to be spared the other thing, as if God were not wise enough to choose for us the best, nor loving enough to give the best to us. Oh, let us abhor and flee from THIS SIN! It is the vilest unbelief, and it dishonours God. We are no more able to know how to choose for our own good, or to wish rightly, than a babe; but we have a matchless

Father to choose for us. Let us trust Him always, and with our whole heart (Ps. lxxxiv. 11 ; Rom. viii. 28).

---

12. TREATED LIKE A FAVOURED PLANT.

How astonishingly good God is to me ! He seems to treat me as a gardener sometimes treats a favoured plant—he puts it into the hot-house, or under a glass cover, and waters it, and airs it, and attends to it constantly. And the Lord deals thus with me. Oh, may He keep me from being like Israel of old, who, after God had done all that could be done with them, when He looked for grapes found only wild grapes (Isa. v. 1–7).

---

13. A DELICATE FOREIGN PLANT.

A WILD weed will grow without any cultivation. Even a coarse, common, home plant, or flower, will thrive well enough without much attention. But a most delicate foreign plant, that can scarcely be kept alive at all in a climate like ours, will perish if it be not fostered with wisdom and the utmost

care. And grace in the heart is always a tender
exotic. It was brought down from heaven to be
planted in the uncongenial soil of earth, and its
health and growth demands the utmost watchfulness.
God tends it, but we must tend it too; for our
neglect shall certainly cause it to droop and languish
(compare 2 Thess. iii. 5 with Jude 21).

---

14. Training the Bird to Sing.

WHEN I was a child we had a neighbour who
was fond of singing-birds. I have a dim recollection
of seeing him training his birds, with their cages
darkened down to a certain pitch. Experience had
taught him that his birds could best execute what
he wanted from them when placed in the dark.
And so does God deal with His children, whom He
is carefully training for sweetest song. He darkens
the cage, that the mind may not be distracted from
the lesson by what the eye sees; thus, many a heart
has been taught to sing to God all the more sweetly
that it was shut out from the glare and glitter of
this world and its pleasures.

15. Stars are seen Best on a Dark and Cloudless Night.

We never see the stars in their fullest brilliancy unless there be a dark night and a cloudless sky. Moonlight will blot out the half of them and more ; while sunshine hides them completely. And so is it, too, with the heavens to which faith lifts up her eyes, for all her delights are there. The stars of this heaven cannot be seen in their full glory unless looked at in a dark, dark night. Earthly prosperity often annihilates them to vision ; and even a very, very small enjoyment of the world's good things makes them often very dim. To those whom men generally count the happy ones, the stars of this heaven shine few in number, and are scarcely visible; but to those who have no light besides, who have nothing to brighten their gloom but GOD and His Christ, oh, how gloriously do these brilliant stars shine forth ! A Lazarus on the pavement sees them in all their beauty, while Dives in his palace cannot catch a glimpse of one. Let my lot be with those who have least of earth and most of heaven.

16. COMMUNION OF LOVE AIMED AT.

GOD delights in the communion of giving love on His side, and of trusting and obedient love on ours ; and we are meant to find in it our very heaven. There is for us no holiness, no happiness, apart from this ; and if our past temporal mercies have not led us into such communion with God, how gracious then is it in Him to withdraw the hurtful comforts, in order that the very want of them may do for us what the supply failed to do.

———

17. GOD'S LOVE GIVES EVERY GOOD THING.

GOD gives us *everything* that would be really good for us—EVERYTHING. He keeps nothing back (Ps. lxxxiv. 11). He grudges us *nothing*. For love, fervent love, never sets bounds to its manifest actions. If the beloved one can be benefited by *anything* that love CAN DO for it, then, no matter how great the trouble or the sacrifice may be, love will never scruple to undertake it. So works *human* love, and so too works *Divine*. Nay, if you point out to a man that what his love sets him upon attempting to do is quite beyond his power, he will still try *his* BEST to do it ; and he will actually do it, if the thing can be done at all. Now, how consoling it is to faith, when it is under trial, to look on the love of God in this light. What manner of love is it (1 John iii. 1)? What has it not done ? What has it not further undertaken to do ? What is it not continually occupied with doing for us ? Oh, let us rejoice with a joy unspeakable in the faith of this, and let us seek to be filled, on our side, with a love to God that shall secure for Him the devoted trust and service of our whole lives.

---

18. CONTENTMENT.

PAUL says, " I have *learned*, in WHATSOEVER state I am, therewith to be CONTENT " (Phil. iv. 11). Oh, with what sweetness this spirit fills the whole soul ! It is our duty as much as it was Paul's duty, and we have precisely the same reasons for it. God is thinking of you and me as surely and as lovingly as He was thinking of Paul (Ps. xl. 17) ; and we must believe that He does so just as Paul believed it. And in learning this lesson of perfect

contentment with the will of God, as well as in
practising it constantly, we have the same sufficient
help that Paul had (ver. 13).   In fact, this is the
grand lesson that our blessed Lord sets every disciple to learn (see carefully Matt. xi. 28–30).
And Paul LEARNED it.   Nobody has got it by
nature.   It must be learned, and learned from
Christ as Teacher.   There is in many a natural
softness and easiness that is counted contentment,
but it is really SLOTH.   True contentment is far
different from this.   It is a grace of the NEW man,
not a mere virtue of the OLD man, and is possible
to one only through Christ strengthening him (see
ver. 13).

And what reasons have we to be thus perfectly
resigned to the holy will of God?   We deserve
nothing, nothing but hell, and may well be overcome with astonishment that we are out of it.   On
the other hand, what has God given us in His love?
He has given us what?   Try to count up His
mercies—you will find they cannot be numbered.
He has given to you and me more, much more, than
He has given to any angel, to ALL the ANGELS in
heaven put together; for He has given us His Son.

And all the circumstances of our earthly lot, every
particular in it, God has planned in His infinite

wisdom, so that the whole shall fit us perfectly, and shall all work together for our very highest good. And for us to fret or be displeased with this arrangement of His is wicked rebellion against Him. Whatever, therefore, may be the trials into which God leads us, let us sweeten them with the assurance of His Fatherly love, and with the most lively hopes of the everlasting glory, and we shall be truly content.

---

19. Careful not to Lose the Benefit of Affliction.

THERE is need to be jealous of our hearts, lest we lose the benefit of a sharp affliction, lest we suffer many things in vain (Gal. iii. 4). This is a grievous loss, a loss with which, alas! I am too well acquainted. Oh, let us dread to incur a loss like this; and we shall not escape it without much watchfulness and prayer. Affliction, by itself, does not by any means secure blessing to the sufferer. I have just been reading in Job ii., and am struck with this, that, while Job was so benefited by the severe trials which were laid on him, in chap. i., his poor wife, who had borne the same, is only

made the worse for them. And we are taught a
similar lesson by the two thieves, crucified with
Jesus; one softened and saved, one hardened and
reviling the Lord to the last. May the Lord bless
ALL your troubles and mine in the FULLEST
MEASURE. Unless He does, they shall profit us
nothing.

----

20. ABUNDANT SUPPLY FOR EVERY TIME OF NEED.

WHEN the hour of *need* comes, the supply of
needed grace shall come with it (2 Cor. xii. 9) ;
when the suffering abounds, the consolation shall
abound with it (2 Cor. i. 5). The suffering child
of God is being led with new experiences, in which
he shall receive new proofs of his Redeemer's
changeless love. His grace is such that, just as it
takes a chief sinner to exhibit adequately the freeness and the fulness of His pardoning mercy, so it
takes a *great grief* to furnish a suitable opportunity
for the display of His abundant consolation.

----

21. Kept in Constant Dependence on Him.

Our Heavenly Father keeps us constantly in the condition of uttermost dependence on Him ; for were it otherwise with us, how wanton would we become. Therefore He writes the sentence of death upon ourselves, and also upon our choicest temporal mercies—not that He always means to remove them, but that He means us, in retaining them, to hold them as a special gift from Him ; and, despairing of all succour but His own, that we should place our trust not on self, nor on valued fellow-creatures, but on God, who can raise up to help us even the very dead (2 Cor. i. 8–10). He is considering our weakness, and our need, and our work ; and in perfect wisdom and love has already arranged for the very best.

---

22. God's Word the Surest of all Certainties.

How much do we walk by sight ; and how little by faith—the very opposite of what we are called to do (2 Cor. v. 7). With perfect faith, our spiritual strength would actually have no bounds

(see Matt. xvii. 20 ; Phil. iv. 13), while our continual joy would be unspeakable (1 Peter i. 8).
But how often is it that our Blessed Lord might
say to us, as He did to the twelve, "Why are ye so
fearful ?   How is it that ye have NO FAITH ?"
We step on the solid rock of God's Word much
as timorous people would venture on thin ice over
deep water, or as one might risk a serious sum of
money in buying a ticket in a lottery, which he
hoped might turn out a prize, but which he thought
was likely to be a blank.   God's promise is no ice,
no lottery ticket—it is the surest of all certainties.
Let our faith be courageous and firm.

---

23. ABRAHAM'S TRIAL.

ON the beloved Isaac of every Abraham, God
lays His hand, and says, " *Give Me this ;* " while
He may allow an Eli to keep his over-loved sons.
And why is Abraham so tried, while Eli is so
spared ?   I fancy it was because Abraham was *an
Abraham*, while Eli was only *an Eli*.   Abraham
had been tried again and again on much smaller
matters, and had stood the trials ; and so he is

honoured by being subjected to this his greatest
trial; but Eli, tried on smaller matters, had completely failed.   And so Eli is spared the heavier
trial—for he would not be able to bear it (1 Cor.
x. 13).   I have said Abraham was HONOURED in
being so severely tried; for when any child of God
endures his appointed trial (James i. 12), the fruits
of it are inexpressibly sweet to God (1 Peter i. 7),
and inexpressibly rich in blessing to the tried man
himself.   He would have been eternally a loser if
he had missed the trial.

---

24. WHAT CHRIST HAS, IS FOR HIS PEOPLE.

WHAT a blessed thing to know that all that
Christ has as the head of the body, the Church
(and in Him dwelleth all the fulness of the Godhead, Col. i. 19; ii. 9), He has it only and
altogether for His people.   Just as the clouds,
which receive and retain their watery treasures, not
for sake of themselves, but that they may empty
all their fulness abundantly on the thirsty ground,
and just as the mother secretes and stores up the
nutritious milk in her breasts, not for her own
nourishment, but to give it *every drop* to her

beloved, helpless child; so Christ, glorified in heaven, is spending ALL that the Father gave Him for the blessing of the beloved body of which He is the Head. For love cannot act otherwise. Love *sacrifices* ITSELF; and it is love only on this condition. Love *cannot,* CANNOT keep to itself anything that would benefit the dearly beloved. Let us ever keep saying to ourselves, "He loved ME, and gave HIMSELF for me" (Gal. ii. 20).

---

25. CHRIST EVERYTHING.

LET Christ be EVERYTHING to you and to me. He fills heaven with its blessedness; shall He not be quite able to fill and to overflow our poor little hearts! Let Him be to us our ALL. " None but Christ, nothing but Christ," let this be the cry of our hearts. Jesus is *something,* more or less, to almost everybody in these lands; nay, He is *much* to a goodly number; but to few is Jesus the ALL IN ALL—the one object of desire and of delight. Let Him be altogether so to you and to me. He is so to those who truly know Him and truly love Him. To those who believe, He is precious. Oh, how precious! I feel that the one grand lesson God has been keeping me at, all these years of suffering, has been the infinite preciousness of Christ, and that His aim has been to lead me to make Christ my all.

---

26. Christ is Ours.

He bore for us on the Cross the awful burden of our sins; and now He bears for us the burden of our cares, our sorrows, our needs of every kind. Let us carry everything to Him. Let His free and most undeserved love sweeten our lives for us. He is *all* ours, our very own, as nothing else is ours; He is ours, with all that is in Him. And what is in Him ? Why, nothing less than all the fulness of the Godhead (Col. ii. 9). Is not that enough for us ? Let us then, by constant exercise of faith, draw strength out of Him to aid our weakness, and joy out of Him to gladden our sorrow, and life out of Him to quicken our death. For He is our very own ; and we are made free to use His stores as such.

CHAPTER XXXIV.

THE THREE JEWS IN THE FURNACE.

WHAT a striking story in Daniel, chapter 3, about the three Jews! One sees that it was a far more wonderful display of Divine power and goodness, to keep them in comfort, in the midst of the sevenfold heated furnace, than to have kept them from it, or to have snatched them out of it. How foolish, then, for us, in our unbelieving dread of suffering, to pray mainly for temporal escape! No, let our cry be that the Son of GOD may be with us in the fierce furnace; and, if He be beside us, not a hair of our heads shall be singed; nay, there shall not be even the smell of fire about us. Is not this infinitely better, more glorifying to God, and more beneficial to ourselves, than if we had been spared the affliction? Alas, alas, what a distressing thing it is to pass through sore affliction, and yet to receive no profiting; to

have God's very bellows turned on us, and the lead
that was meant to help the melting, all consumed,
but the heart will not be melted (Jer. vi. 28, 30).
There are other sufferers, again, who, if they ever
come out of the fire, come out burnt, so far from
having no smell of fire about them, they smell of
nothing else. Everything about them indicates
not only that they have been sorely afflicted, but
that they have lost all that they cared for, in the
furnace. The Romish saints, according to Romish
fable, are said to be known by a certain mark;
their bodies, even in the grave, gave out a
fragrant smell. Well, I don't believe it; but
I do believe that God's saints, chosen by Him
in the furnace, should bear about with them a
very special smell of heaven, but not the smallest
scent of burning.

As a spiritual discipline, sanctified suffering is
inestimably precious — nothing helps growth in
grace so much; let us then welcome it heartily,
assured that God has some new sweet lesson to
teach us by it, some rich and priceless gift of love,
of which He makes it the bearer. And the pain
which it inflicts is not harmful; it is, at worst,
but the tight squeeze of our Father's loving
embrace, as He clasps His darling child closer to

His heart. What a trifle is the pain of the pressure, when we sweeten it with this thought!

It is by suffering that we are perfected (1 Peter i. 7). It is not by outward comforts that sinners are brought to God, nor are saints made more Christlike, more holy, or more happy, by their outward ease (Rev. vii. 14).

And besides the profit, affliction, when we have Christ with us in the furnace, never abates a believer's true happiness. It both purifies and multiplies his joy. At the present moment, GOD is bringing the very sweetest music that rises to Him in praise out of created lips, from most sorely afflicted sufferers. But in order to this, the pegs need ofttimes to be screwed very tightly indeed, to bring up the chords of the instrument to the proper pitch. But, be sure, the Great Musician shall not screw them too tight; much less till the string breaks. But the tuning is indispensable, for slack strings cannot give forth full, clear, sweet notes. Let us leave the tuning of us, then, entirely to Himself, rejoicing when He takes us up to bring us into such harmony as shall be fitted to pour forth the most enrapturing music, not only on earth, and now, but still more in heaven, and for evermore.

In view of these, and of many other still

weightier considerations, should not our patience, as children of God under His afflicting hand, be something that cannot fail to astonish and awe the beholders? Like Nebuchadnezzar, when he saw the miracle of the three Jews, should not a Christian's patience be such as to constrain men to feel: "This is more than nature; God of a truth is here." We read of the patience of Job, but there was much dross in it; our patience ought to go far beyond his; it ought to be free from dross, since our light is, beyond comparison, so much clearer than his, and our helps so much superior.

But I am ashamed to have used the word patience in connection with this subject. I can understand, in a way, God's wonderful patience with me, and am astounded at it; but to speak of my patience, PATIENCE with GOD, the ALL-WISE and ALL-LOVING, seems impious. Nay, O my God, help me always to rejoice in the loving strokes of Thy healing hand, and, when Thou art pleased to smite me, may I be enabled to cover Thy smiting hand, nay, the rod that it uses, with my most grateful kisses.

CHAPTER XXXV.

DEATH.

1. To Die is Gain.

WE should not desire either a sudden death, or exemption from it, but we should desire and pray for perfect readiness whenever the Lord may call. And He gives me to feel in general with dear old Isaac Watts, "I bless God that I can lie down with comfort at night, not being anxious whether I shall wake in this world or in the other."

What solemn lessons has death got to teach us of the utter vanity of the world's things, of the enormity of sin as God looks at it; and what a sweet lesson, too, it has to teach us of the matchless love of Jesus, who, for our sakes, became obedient unto that king of terrors, even death. Long ago, when I used to be often beside the dying, I liked to watch the last struggle, in order

that the sight might burn in these lessons,
especially the last of them, on my heart. We die,
because we cannot escape it ; but He was born, just
that He might DIE. Herein is love.

Among my many mercies, one has been that
God has never permitted me to forget death. And
now I feel as if intimately familiar with it — he is
a companion, a friend ; indeed, he is not death at
all. Oh, what an immeasurable difference there is
between the death of a Christian and that of the
unforgiven ; between death as administered by the
gentle hands of the loving Saviour (1 Thess. iv. 14),
and as administered by the Devil, acting as God has
commissioned (Heb. ii. 14).

I have often hung with joy and wonder over
the strong words in 2 Tim. i. 10, "Who hath
ABOLISHED death"—that is, put it out of existence
altogether. Yes, dear friend, for the Christian
there is now no longer any death ; and it is
because our faith is so very feeble that so many of
us are in fear of it. To the Christless, it is the
sum of all horrors, but to the man in Christ, it is
the bringer of inconceivable blessedness. For him,
death has no sting (1 Cor. xv. 55). It left its
poison-sting in the body of the Lord Jesus. It is
now not death, but SLEEP. To die is gain.

Blessed are the dead that die in the Lord; they depart to be with Christ, which is far better. Oh, let us live as befits those who look on death as belonging to them, and not as if they belonged to death; who know that the day of death is sure to be better than the day of birth (1 Cor. iii. 22; Eccles. vii. 1). Baxter spoke of his dying day as "My third birthday"—a day to be thought of and spoken about with gladness.

The dying hour is very solemn, but the living hour is every whit just as solemn; and we shall feel it to be so, if we walk constantly with GOD. We would be shocked to see a man die amid heartless frivolities—why are we not equally shocked to see him live among them? Where is the difference?

The death-bed is the fitting sequel to the life, and may be expected to be of a piece with it. It is the result of the living—just as the crop reaped in harvest is of the same nature as the seed sown in spring (see Gal. vi. 7, 8).

Oh, let us see that we are living in and for Christ, and then we may be sure that to die is gain.

2. SHRINKING FROM DEATH.

THE shrinking from death is natural to man; and one has no warrant to say that, even in the Christian, it is sinful. But vigorous faith easily overcomes the reluctance of nature; and it seems to indicate a low degree of spiritual vigour when the Christian recoils from thoughts of *dying—to be with Christ*, which is far better than any life here can be. He cannot have a very profound conviction of the horrors and enormities of sin who draws back from the sinless life above, and would rather continue here. But I don't think it lawful for any one to choose for himself, either to live or to die. Let us leave such arrangements to our Father, and let us be ready to welcome His blessed will, whatever it brings.

Death is completely changed to the genuine believer, however feeble his faith may be. To him death is ABOLISHED—that is, there is no longer in his case any death at all (2 Tim. i. 10). It is not DEATH; it is the Father's messenger of love to fetch home his worn-out child. But there are not a few who apprehend very imperfectly how the Lord Jesus has DESTROYED him that had the power of death, and who therefore continue, through this needless fear of death, to be all their lifetime subject to bondage (Heb. ii. 14). How gently and how tenderly should such timid ones be handled! If I were speaking to any one of this class, I would like to remind him of his own past experiences of God's loving care. I would ask: Has He not led thee through many sore trials, and has He ever forsaken thee in any one of them? Nay, has He not made His grace so to abound towards thee, that His faithful love has made thee ashamed of thine unbelieving fears? Trust Him still. Death is only the child's last step in his journey HOME; and his Father, who has all along been with him, shall be specially with him now. Death is the believer's LAST trial, and ofttimes it is among his LIGHTEST. Looked at by faith it is scarcely a trial at all.

CHAPTER XXXVI.

OUR BLESSED LORD'S SPEEDY RETURN.

I AM happy that you see so clearly the prominent place which in Scripture is assigned to the important and stimulating truth of our Blessed Lord's speedy return in glory. May the same Divine Spirit who has filled His inspired Word with the vivifying theme, keep our hearts equally filled with it.

For myself, I find that it is much easier to have the mind exercised with the doctrine and its fascinating details, and to have the mere emotions stirred occasionally by it, than to have the heart, with all its affections, permanently engrossed with the sanctifying exercises of a truly spiritual hope, occupied with the person of the expected Beloved One Himself. It was for this practical use of it that this truth has been revealed to us, and it serves no profitable purpose whatever, except in so far as the faith of it constitutes one of the mightiest motive powers in our actual living from day to day.

And we need the powerful help of this "blessed hope." How ready are we to forget our stranger-hood on earth, to allow ourselves to be snared so far by the attractions of a forsaken world, and the still powerful lustings of a nature that we have nailed to the Cross (Gal. v. 24), and the wiles of the great deceiver who actually deceives the whole world! But everything about us is seen in its true colours, while we are enabled to attain and to maintain this characteristic attitude of waiting for our Lord. The world's attractions are all disenchanted in a moment, and the world's sorrows are felt to be beneath our notice, when we vividly realise that the "Coming of our Lord" is at hand, and have the foretastings which faith even now gives us of the grace which shall be revealed at "His appearing" (1 Peter i. 3).

For Christ is our *absolute* ALL. He is our very life (Col. iii. 3), and all that this better life is capable of enjoying. Earth can now give us no satisfaction. It is a dry and thirsty land, without one droplet of water (Ps. lxiii. 1). Where, then, can we turn for indispensably-needed solace but to believing, expectant thoughts of Him whose promised coming we look for and vehemently desire, and whose love is better to us than wine (Song of Sol. i. 2, 4). Indeed, this hope of His coming has been given to us that we may refresh ourselves in the weariness of our pilgrim journey with frequent sips of this wine of the kingdom (2 Sam. xvi. 2).

> " For I am weaker than a child,
>   And Thou art more than mother dear ;
>   Without Thee, heaven were but a wild—
>   How could I live without Thee here ? "

And then this " blessed hope," when it is genuine, does not interfere with, but on the contrary, greatly helps the maintenance of a present communion. As one fragment of revealed truth never casts another into the shade, but each one serves to set all the rest in clearer light, so one part of the Holy Spirit's work on a soul deepens and strengthens all the rest. Hence, hope makes faith more believing, and love more fervent, and self-denial more decided, and present communion with our Head more lively. And we are rightly exercising this hope only as we are being led by it into the holy joys of a present fellowship. I do believe that there is far more of the elements of a present heaven within our reach than most of us ever think. Let our hope then excite our spiritual desires to the uttermost, to seek, in the fullest measure attainable, the sanctifying joys of a present communion. With His Spirit ever in our hearts to make our communion with Him possible, and to draw us to seek it; with Himself present in every ordinance, nay, in every incident of life, and present, too, just that we may have unbroken communion with Him—should not life be to us henceforward like what the Holy of Holies was to the Jewish High Priest? May He enable us to make it such. Wherever our persons may be, may we be, in spirit, beneath our apple tree, enjoying that communion which is so sweet to us, but which is sweeter far to Him.